The Blessed Virgin
According to the Gospels

Readings and Stories for Each Day
of the Month of Mary

By the Rev. Marin de Boylesve, S. J.

Translated and Annotated
by E.A. Bucchianeri

The Blessed Virgin
According to the Gospels

Readings and Stories for Each Day
of the Month of Mary

By the Rev. Marin de Boylesve, S.J.

Translated and Annotated
by E.A. Bucchianeri

Batalha Publishers
Fatima, Portugal

This first English translation edition is based on the 1883 edition published by René Haton of Paris. The translation, added biography of the author, annotations and appendix by E.A. Bucchianeri, © 2022 by Batalha Publishers, Portugal.

ISBN: 978-989-53726-0-7

Table of Contents

ॐ ❀ ॐ

ഇ❀ങ

Hymns

ഇ ✿ ര

APPENDIX

About this Edition

This edition has been translated from the French edition published by René Hatton, Paris (1883) and features British spelling. Also includes new material not in the original, such as the biography of the author, annotations, illustrations, and the devotions in the Appendix.

E.A. Bucchianeri

About the Author

Fr. Marin de Boylesve was born on November 28, 1813 at the Château de la Coltrie in the commune of Saint-Lambert de la Potherie near Angers. He came from a distinguished aristocratic family whose name can be traced back many centuries as seen in Abbé Jean-Baptiste Ladvocat's *Dictionnaire historique portatif* (1755). Fr. Marin descended directly from Eslienne Boyliaue (or Boilyeve), the great statesman and the principal adviser of St. Louis IX, King of France. Other illustrious ancestors included intrepid knights, one in particular also named Marin joined the cause of King Henry IV. After the Battle of Arques, the king called him 'his beloved knight', granted him a heredity knighthood in 1597, then was made Seigneur de la Maurouziere in 1598 thereby granting him the right to add three gold fleur-de-lis to the top of his arms and bear the signs of the Order of St. Michel in his escutcheon. He was also appointed lieutenant-general of Anjou and councillor of state as a reward for his dedication. Another Marin Boylesve appears in the family line, the third to hold the name, and was in service to King Louis XIV as manager of his hôtel. Loyal to the French King and to their Catholic faith, many members of the family were forced to emigrate during the French Revolution, but some members stayed behind in their beloved France. Fr. de Boylesve would recall a favourite family story, of how his grandmother was imprisoned in Angers by the Revolutionaries and managed a daring escape on the road during a prisoner transfer to the local castle.

While she pretended to pick up a dropped package, a solider kicked her into the ditch. She took the opportunity to flee to a nearby house. However, when they threatened to imprison those harbouring escaped prisoners, she bravely marched straight in to the Revolutionary Office and gave herself up to ensure the safety of those who sheltered her. The revolutionaries did not dare risk upsetting the populace as her father was the former mayor of Angers before the Revolution and loved by the people. They decided to let her return to her father's house.

Fr. de Boylesve was the last direct descendant of his distinguished line, having followed the call to enter the Company of Jesus, or Jesuits, which also is a remarkable story of a predestined vocation. The Jesuits were persecuted due to fears they were growing in power and wealth. Pressured by the royal courts of Europe, Pope Clement XIV suppressed the Society, forcing members of the order to renounce their vows and go into exile. They were expelled from France in 1764. Fr. de Boylesve's mother, Clémentine de Livonnière, made a solemn promise on the day of her wedding that if God permitted the Jesuits to return to France and she was granted a son, she would offer him to the order and entrust him to it. As mentioned, Fr. Marin was born in 1813, a year before 1814 when Pope Pius VII restored the Society. Tragedy struck when Marin's father died, Marin was only ten months old at the time, but keeping her promise his mother dutifully sent him for his education at the age of ten to the Jesuit Fathers of Montmorillon. The moment he arrived at the school and saw a Jesuit for the first time who happened to be the Superior of the college Fr. Michel Le Blanc, he heard an inner voice say to him: "Little one, that is what you will be."

Fr. de Boylesve entered the school as a student and was destined never to leave the Jesuits. In 1831 he turned eighteen, a year after the July Revolution of 1830, which saw the rightful king to the French throne Charles X overthrown. His heir, Henry V the 'Miracle Child', was forced into exile at the age of ten, his throne usurped by the man who had been approached to be his regent, Louis-Philippe, Duke of Orléans. The events of the times burned the hearts of the faithful as the historical church of the royal family, Saint-Germain-l'Auxerrois, was profaned. Paris was sacked, and wayside devotional crosses and shrines over large areas of France were destroyed as Catholic legitimist symbols of Charles X, even those which had no royal significance or connection to the king.

Fr. Marin had just completed his schooling when he formally announced his decision to enter the Society, the historic events of the previous year and their aftermath no doubt influencing his decision. Writing to his grandmother he declared: "The course of my studies completed I could not remain without doing anything. God will ask us for an exact account of all the moments He gives us. Full of this thought I ardently wished to serve my country and the Church especially. At a time when both are in such great peril, as a Frenchman and as a Christian, I felt the need to throw myself into the thick of the fray. To take place in the first rows under the banners of religion whose triumph alone can bring glory and happiness back to my homeland, to serve immediately under my first head Jesus Christ, to be one of His companions, seemed to me the most glorious at the same time as most useful for my neighbour. Immense advantages, treasures of happiness and glory, the hundredfold from this life of all that I would give to the Lord, all of these promised in the gospel by Jesus Christ, strongly attracted me to be generous. What more could I do than give myself? (...)"

His family strongly opposed, especially as he was the last direct heir to the Boylesve house, but his mother let him go despite the great sacrifice, no doubt she understood God was accepting her promise to give him to the Jesuits, and not just for his education but now was asking for his whole life, a bitter dreg for her down to the last drop of the cup.

He entered the Novitiate in 1831 at Estavayer in the canton of Fribourg in Switzerland with two other students. As they arrived at their new school, they rang the doorbell at the moment the house clock struck three. The Father who received them remarked: "You are entering at the hour of the Sacred Heart." This introduction to a new school would once again give Fr. de Boylesve a sign regarding the future work he would one day accomplish, although on this occasion he did not know it at the time. He made his first vows at the Maison du Passage on October 10, 1833. He studied philosophy and then in 1835 became a supervisor at the Collège de Mélan, a position he held for one year. He remained in the same college until 1842 where he was in succession professor of grammar, humanities and rhetoric. He thoroughly enjoyed his work with the students, writing in 1837:

"I find this job a lot of fun, despite the hardships that come with it. I have forty students; I love them and I try to spare nothing to make them good Christians, educated Christians capable of one day rendering true service to religion and to the state. It is the sight of such a noble ending that sustains and animates me." In the same letter he continues, regarding his concern for his family, "(...) what the only important thing is, is everyone behaving well and does he remember the motto of the family, RELIGIO, PATRIA? For me who gave up everything, even my name which will be extinguished in my person, I remember it, and God grant that I am consumed and that I use myself in the service of one and of the other."

Although renouncing his aristocratic life he never gave up its noble spirit represented by the family motto, an ardent loyalty to the Catholic faith of his forefathers and his country. In the title pages of his texts he included the family crest of three crosses and motto: RELIGIO, PATRIE – "Faith and Country". Those who knew him and his 'military' style ways said he was just like the loyal intrepid knights of old.

At the end of 1842 he returned to France. He took theology courses at Laval for four years. Instinctively he was drawn to the writings of St. Thomas Aquinas and steered clear of new systems that deviated from the philosophical teachings of the Seraphic Doctor. In 1846 theology training completed, Fr. Boylesve was sent by his superiors to Angers, then in his third year at Notre-Dame d'Ay. In 1848 he was appointed to Brugelette, where he occupied the chair of philosophy. One student who fondly recalled Fr. de Boylesve and his time at Brugelette said his arrival was providential. His classes were easy to follow his manner clear and crisp, but this is not all that gained the respect of the students. In 1848 they were restless as revolution was in the air, Louis-Philippe I, who had overthrown Catholic King Charles X was now in his own turn overthrown. Rising above and beyond what was required of his philosophy courses, Fr. Boylesve seized the opportunity like a knight-commander of old to direct the lazy students yet bursting with energy towards something constructive: Catholic action to fashion them into vigorous young men of service for Church and country. With his apostolic action he captivated the students with his literature classes, speaking on many subjects from philosophy, history, politics both ancient and modern. He particularly drew them with his catechism lessons on the Council of Trent, his clarity and enthusiasm captivating them.

As Fr. de Boylesve loved his students he was equally admired and loved by them, earning the nickname 'The Captain' as a mark of respect. The students composed a military style tune for his birthday, the refrain remaining popular and hummed everywhere: "Courageous Captain, lead us into battle." A student recalls: "I understood all that was apostolic about his action on us. We can sum it up by saying that he made it his mission to preach to us always and everywhere the contemplation of Saint Ignatius on the Reign of Jesus Christ as it is given in the Exercises." In 1851 Fr. Boylesve was sent to Vannes where he was made prefect of studies, his nickname 'The Captain' following him. In October 1853 he left the post and resumed teaching philosophy, a position that he would keep for a long time, either in Poitiers or in Vaugirard.

Known to be quiet and reserved when on his own, it was another matter when he was teaching or publicly speaking. He was incapable of remaining silent or softening his direct manner of expression when it was a question of truth, and did not hold back when it came to defend the Faith and the Church against unbelievers, becoming as noted like his knight-ancestor of old, charging forth to give chase and defeat any bold rascal on the field of battle albeit with his tongue and writings rather than with a literal sword. His attitude is quaintly summed up by the art critique he once gave of the statue of the fountain of St. Michael in Paris, complaining with slight annoyance that the mighty archangel was made to look too carefree and benevolent when dispatching Satan: "See then, it is that he seems to spare him!" He was also a zealous worker and relished activity. He once wrote: "I challenge my superiors to give me too much work." In addition to his religious duties and teaching, he was a prolific writer, his output seeming to have no end. He wrote on a myriad of subjects and in different genres, from devotional booklets and pamphlets to history, literature, philosophy, Biblical dramas, summaries of the Church Fathers and Doctors, his own sermons, studies of the Scriptures, Our Lady, of which this book is just one example, the Exercises of St. Ignatius just to name a few, there were always more plans for further works in progress, his room filled with notes and notebooks. He was always studying as well, also making it a practise to read through the entire Bible every year. One might call him a workaholic in today's terms, but it was noted he believed in a time and a place for everything and diligently managed his hours. He enjoyed recreation time, especially going for walks, and did not sacrifice rest. Despite his zest for work, he disapproved of a few young professors who sacrificed too much sleep and recreation time for their studies, endangering their health. Yet, while sparing of his time, he was ever charitable and ready to help another all for the glory of God.

In September 1870 Fr. de Boylesve was sent to the College of Le Mans, Notre-Dame de Sainte-Croix, when the Franco-Prussian war was raging and France suffered the indignity of invasion. The humiliation felt by the country also struck the pious and patriotic Fr. de Boylesve to the core: "I searched through the memories of my life; I do not remember ever having felt greater pain than this, not even when I learned of my mother's death. This humiliation of France, the Eldest Daughter of the Church, thus succumbing before Prussia, the Eldest Daughter of Protestantism, in the face of the whole world, is something unheard of."

The Messenger, the magazine of the Apostleship of Prayer run by the Jesuits, began spreading the visions of St. Margaret Mary, declaring the only way France would be saved from her enemies was to embrace the devotion to the Sacred Heart. The message inspired Fr. de Boylesve. He became a chaplain to the Catholic Papal Zouaves forces sent to defend the French Motherland from the Protestant invaders, giving them rousing sermons: "Clotilde, inspiring faith in Clovis, saved the Franks and slaughtered the Germans at their feet ... Joan of Arc by her standard delivered France from the English! Your standard is the Sacred Heart." The Zouaves placed the Sacred Heart on their banner. Fr. de Boylesve also busily spread Sacred Heart badges of wool for the soldiers to pin on their uniforms, for they were in high demand. A gifted and inspiring preacher, his sermons encouraged them onward, even when they were driven back in defeat by the Prussians to where the soldiers remarked: "This man can lead us to the fire tomorrow; we would gladly be killed for him."

Fr. de Boylesve is fondly remembered today in Catholic circles in France for his work as the director of the Apostleship of Prayer in Le Mans through which he contributed to the spread of devotion to the Sacred Heart. On October 17, 1870 Fr. de Boylesve was appointed to preach at the Visitation of Le Mans upon St. Margaret Mary for his subject, who at the time was a Blessed. He also preached upon another mystic who had died within their own times, Mother Marie de

Jesus (1797-1854) from the convent des Oiseaux of Paris who had received revelations from the Sacred Heart that were favourably recognised by the Archbishop of Paris. On June 21, 1823 the Sacred Heart revealed to Sr. Marie that He desired France be consecrated to His Sacred Heart by the King, and that a chapel be built and dedicated to Him, and the feast of the national consecration be formally celebrated every year. "After my sermon," recounts Fr. Boylesve, "the Mother Superior expressed to me her astonishment at my silence with regard to an almost similar order that Our Lord had given to Blessed Margaret Mary on June 17th, 1689. I confessed that in our college, which had barely opened for a month, I had not found the letters of the Blessed One and that I was unaware of the apparition and the order she was telling me about. I promised to make good this omission." Apparently at that time, the Sacred Heart's requests to St. Margaret Mary for a shrine and the national consecration of France by the King were not yet widely known.

True to his word, filled with his characteristic zeal for faith and country, doing what he could to extend the reign of Jesus Christ through his beloved homeland and secure its safety, the very next day he repaired his omission by publishing a pamphlet featuring the prophecies of St. Margaret Mary and Mother Marie de Jesus entitled "Triumph of France by the Sacred Heart", composing a special prayer of consecration to be said, which the Zouaves said every Friday as hope in the Sacred Heart was sorely needed. Paris was threatened with destruction by bombardments, then starvation by the invading Prussians, having commenced a siege around the city in September 1870. The siege continued until January 1871, the citizens reduced to dire circumstances. The zoo animals were slaughtered for food, the populace also living off of stray animals and rats. While the Prussian advance had ceased, humiliation still ensued when France suffered defeat at the hands of the Prussians with the establishment of the German Empire, also losing the territory of the Alsace-Lorraine to the victors. The troubles were not over. From March to May 1871 Paris fell into the clutches of the anticlerical socialist Communards, rebels revolting against the new government of the Third Republic. Blood ran in the streets, historical buildings burned, including the Tuileries Palace. The anticlerical Communards also executed the Archbishop of Paris, Georges Darboy, fulfilling the prophecy of St. Catherine Laboure. This horrific turn of events, combined with the circulation of prophecies foretelling the destruction of Paris was at hand, the faithful no doubt felt doom hung over the city. The times were desperate. After several reprintings, including a full reproduction of the text by Fr. Ramiere in the 'Messenger' newsletter issued by the Apostleship of Prayer, more than 330,000 copies of Fr. de Boylesve's pamphlets of the 'Triumph of the Sacred Heart' were circulated. It contributed to the rapid spread devotion to the Sacred Heart and bolstered the call to have the Universal Church consecrated to the Sacred Heart, also to build a national shrine on Montmartre in atonement for the atrocities committed by the Communards who began their uprising there. Construction began in 1875, the cornerstone was laid on June 16, 1875, the day Bl. Pius IX encouraged all the faithful to pray the consecration to the Sacred Heart using the special formula composed by the Sacred Congregation of Rites for the 200th anniversary of the apparition of the Sacred to St. Margaret Mary. The construction of Sacre Coeur was at last completed in 1914.

As for Fr. de Boylesve, in addition to his efforts to spread devotion to the Sacred Heart of Jesus, he worked unceasingly at many other endeavours, not only as director of the Apostolate of Prayer in Le Mans, but also with the Confraternities of Saint Joseph such as that of the Good Death, and also the Confraternity of the Agonizing Heart, the Work of Campaigns, Conferences of St. Vincent de Paul, Workers' Circles. He still appeared to dare all and sundry that they would never be able to find enough work for him to do. He amazed all that he was never at a loss for a subject to preach upon. He could easily vary his sermons to where it appeared he never preached the same way twice, and always captured his hearers' attention. One day out of curiosity a hardened sinner walked in to listen to him preach and left a converted man. When Fr. Boylesve wasn't working, he was praying. There was no question that he maintained a deep spiritual life.

He was transferred to Vaugirard in 1875, returning to Le Mans two years later in 1877. Three years later his teaching came to an end at the college there with the decree of March 29, 1880 issued by the French minister for public education prohibiting the Jesuits from engaging in their educational apostolate, only the first of several anticlerical laws that would be passed in France over the next decades. Fr. Boylesve admitted he was on the verge of tears saying his last Mass for the students in the chapel before the school closed. Yet, he remained as active as ever despite this terrible blow, preaching, giving catechisms and continuing his writing, tackling the problems of their day threatening both the Church and society.

He continued working despite his old age, until the end of 1891 when his activity was curtailed. He was struck with various ailments, first a tormenting dermatitis that remained with him, then inflammation of the blood that restricted his activities for many weeks, although he managed to say Mass and continue his writing, until at last he was struck with paralysis, unable to walk or speak. Clutching his rosary and his crucifix, the ever zealous 'priest-knight' of the Vendée gave up his soul to God in February 22, 1892 and was buried in the Jesuit cemetery of Sainte-Croix.[1]

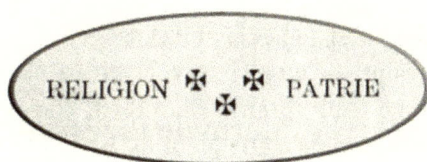

RELIGION ✠ ✠ ✠ PATRIE

---

1   Biographical information from 'Necrologie. Le Père Marin de Boylesve, in 'Lettres de Jersey', Vol.XII, No. 1 (April 1893)

Preface

We present here the life of the Blessed Virgin according to the Gospel, shared in thirty one readings which can serve as nourishment for the piety of the faithful during the Month of Mary, and also during the preparatory Novenas to her main feasts.[+]

The series of historical tracts offers a gallery of the most illustrious saints for their devotion to Mary or for the favours they have received from the divine Mother.[*]

(Fr. Marin de Boylesve, S.J.)

[+]   Fr. de Boylesve does not specify the month. Considering there are 31 reflections, not only is this devotional perfect for Mary's month of May, but all months with 31 days with major feast days of the Blessed Virgin, such as March for the Annunciation, August for the Assumption, and October for the feast of the Holy Rosary. Of course, this book may be read any time of the year, spiritual readings about the Blessed Virgin are efficacious at all times.

[*]   'Divine' Mother: i.e. an expression often found in French texts with the understanding Our Lady is not Divine herself, but Mother of the Divine, and therefore she was granted divine graces unlike those given to any other saint.

The Blessed Virgin According to the Gospels

1. Mary in the Divine Plan

When an architect meditates upon the plan of a building, of a palace for example, or of a temple, the first object of thought will be the throne if it is a palace, and if it is a temple it will be the altar. In second place yet above all the rest comes the throne room for the palace, while for the temple it is the sanctuary. Then the artist draws the plan of the whole edifice, relating all the parts of the palace to the throne room and thereby to the throne and to the king himself, while all the parts of the temple refer to the sanctuary, and thereby to the altar and to God.

Thus from all eternity the Supreme Artist fixed the plan of a palace and a temple of which He is the King and where He is God. The Throne in this palace, the Altar in this temple, is God made man, Jesus Christ. Also, whether by virtue of the foresight of original sin or independently of this fall, the Incarnation being the highest outward manifestation of the glory of God, we can say that it is the primary object, the centre, the final part of the Divine Plan.

In the Eternal Decrees it was decided that the God-Man would be born of a daughter of Adam, and that this girl chosen among all would be the Virgin Mary; therefore in this palace, in this temple of Creation of which angels and men are the living stones,

Mary is like the throne room or the sanctuary, and through her everything from the atom to the seraph relates to Jesus Christ, Who alone by His humanity is the Throne of supreme Kingship, the Altar of the thrice Holy Divinity. Such is the rank that Mary occupies in the Eternal Plan of Creation, the first after her Divine Son. With Him she can say again: 'The Lord possessed me in His foreknowledge, in His decree, at the beginning of His ways, of His thoughts, of His eternal designs.' *Dominus possedit me in initio viarum suarum.* (Prov. 8:22) Let us conclude with St. Anselm: "Everything that exists is above or below Mary: God alone above, all simple creatures below;" as with St. Bonaventure, "God can create a larger world, a sky higher than the world and of the heavens that exist, but He cannot raise a single creature higher than the one of whom He made His Mother." For, as Albert the Great states, "the dignity of the Mother of God is immediately after that of God Himself," and, "Mary cannot be more united to God than she is, unless she becomes God." (Id.) Also, "such is the greatness of Mary," according to St. Bernardine, "that only God can understand it."

Everything in the world relates to Jesus Christ; everything is an announcement of Jesus Christ. Before He came everything prepared and showed it; after His coming everything is a continuation and imitation of His life and His action; in the same way, everything in the world relates to Mary, either to announce her or to remind of her.

Now in this palace and in this temple we also have a marked place. If by His humanity Jesus Christ is the Throne of this palace, the Altar of this temple, if Mary is the throne room and the sanctuary, we must form the rest of the building: *Superaedificati super fundamentum apostolorum.* (Eph. 2:19) (Built upon the foundation of the apostles.) *Quae domus sumus nos.* (Heb. 3: 6) (Which house are we.)

Take care. The stone that does not respond to the architect's design is thrown into the rubble. If there is any work, any word, any thought which does not conform to the required measure, which does not relate to God through Jesus and to Jesus through Mary, that act is lost; for there is no place for him in this palace, in this temple which is called here below the Church, and above, Heaven. Such is the law. From the first *fiat*, from the *fiat lux*, (Be light made), to the *fiat mihi secundum verbum tuum*, (Be it done to me according to thy word), from the Creation to the Last Judgement, everything in the world as well as in man, everything in the public life of nations as well as in the private life of individuals, everything must relate to God through Jesus Christ, and to Jesus Christ through Mary.

The Angels and Mary

One day Saint Michael weighed in the scales the merits of a servant of Mary. The weight of sins prevailed. So Mary threw her client's rosary on the balance and the merits gained the advantage.[2] It is

2   Apparently, this is a story of a person who was devoted Mary who died and went to their particular judgement. According to Tradition, St. Michael holds the scales that weighs our good deeds against our sins when we are tried before God after death. The person who died had too many sins, but Mary stepped forward on behalf of the soul devoted to her and placed their rosary beads on the scales - the merits of all the rosaries that were said during that person's lifetime

believed that it was St. Michael who on Assumption Day led all the angelic legions to meet the Queen of Heaven. (*St. Gregory of Tours*).

St. Gabriel, the Archangel, after having greeted Mary in the name of God Who sent him, announces to her that she will give birth to a son, who will be the Son of the Most High and Whose reign will have no end. Mary, reassured regarding her virginity, gives the example of the most profound humility: 'Behold,' said she, 'the handmaid of Lord'; and in the fullest obedience, added: 'Be it done unto me according to thy word.'

O happy Archangel who was appointed to commence this admirable panegyric which so many mouths would continue to repeat through the ages! Guardian angel of the Mother of God, he was her inseparable companion. (*St. Irenaeus*)

80 ✿ ○8

---

outweighed the crimes committed.

2. She Shall Crush Thy Head

Why did God command not to eat of all the fruits in the garden? — A question as insane as it is insolent when it is addressed to God. God is Wisdom: He knows what is right for me and what is not right for me. God is Goodness: whether He commands or defends, He only wants what is for my good. God is Power: He will know how to punish disobedience.

The serpent continues: 'The day you eat of this fruit, your eyes will be opened and you will be like gods, knowing good and evil.' You do not believe, O men! You do not obey; you do not believe, you do not obey God nor them who represent Him here below. Then, knowing for yourselves what is good, what is bad, what is good for you, what is bad for you, each one of you will rule by himself; you will be independent, you will be like gods: *eritis sicut dii.* Even today, isn't this what all the echoes of the serpent say again?

Eve allowed herself to be seduced. Adam succumbed out of complacency. Instantly there took place in their person a frightful revolution. The soul has rebelled against God; the flesh rebelled against the soul, the senses rise against the intelligence, passion blinds reason and draws freedom[3] towards low and vile things.

The work of Satan is sin. His masterpiece was original sin. Raising up pride and flattering sensuality, the first liar led our first parents into disobedience. They ate of the forbidden fruit and they lost the life of the soul and the life of the body, the paradise of the

---

3   I.e. their free will was weakened and now drawn to lower things.

earth and the paradise of the heavens.

Pride and sensuality, such as they are, even today, are the sources of all our faults and also of all our misfortunes. When will our eyes be opened to recognize by its effects the too real action of the words of the serpent always present, always speaking, always acting in the serpent-scribe and in the serpent-orator, in the sophist and in the libertine of the age?

Adam lost for himself and for us this original grace and justice that he was to transmit to us. Men would thenceforth be born children of wrath: *filii irae*. The generations, succeeding one another like the waves of a river, will be lost in the abyss. Not all men will fall into the Hell of the reprobates, but there is not one for whom Heaven is not closed.[4]

To whom will it be given to escape the universal current, the empire of Satan and the law of sin? God said to the serpent: 'I will put enmity between you and

---

[4]   Fr. de Boylesve is referring to the effects of original sin in that Heaven was closed for a long time to all mankind. While not all men would be damned to Hell, no one was permitted to enter Heaven either – mankind would have been doomed to be excluded from Heaven, the just souls sent to Limbo for all eternity had God not been merciful and promised Redemption. Described as a place between Heaven and Hell, St. Augustine speculated whether Limbo was a level of Hell as it still is a place where souls do not enjoy the Eternal Beatific Vision of the Trinity, and therefore was a place separated from God to an extent. Also, we see there are two 'hells' in theological language - the 'hell' or underworld of the souls awaiting the coming of the Messiah, and the 'hell' of the damned, hence Limbo was considered to be a place on the outskirts or next to Hell: notice in the Apostles Creed it is said Christ 'descended into Hell', that is, after the crucifixion He went to release the just souls bound there. This is no doubt why Fr. de Boylesve declared all men were doomed to fall into the 'abyss', even the just souls, were it not for the promise of the Redemption.

the Woman, between your seed and hers; and she will crush your head.' A Woman will come, therefore, who will be preserved from the disastrous alliance that our first parents had contracted with the infernal spirit. A Son of the Woman will be the enemy of the serpent-race, that is to say of sin. The Woman and her Son will crush the head of the infernal dragon. What is this head, if it is not the sin which was the beginning and the source of all the other sins, if it is not original sin? Hate that sin of that vigorous hatred, which leaves the enemy neither peace nor truce.[5] Pursue sin everywhere, but first and foremost in yourself, until you have crushed the serpent's head in your heart, I mean to say, your dominant fault.

The Parents of Mary

St. Joachim, father of the most Blessed Virgin, loved her as the best of fathers should love the most lovable daughter. But when at the age of three Mary desired to consecrate herself to God, he knew how to

---

5   "Haïssez le péché de cette haine vigoureuse, qui ne laisse à l'ennemi ni paix, ni trêve." An odd expression to translate – what is probably meant here is 'hate' the original sin with a holy hatred, justly 'hate' that sin which was brought about by the vigorous hatred of Satan for the human race and which gives him no peace or truce, for the enmity between the Seed of the Woman and of the Serpent continues in the struggle for the eternal salvation of souls. Fr. de Boylesve then goes on to say by 'pursue', we must hunt down and fight against sin everywhere, first and foremost in ourselves by overcoming our predominant fault.

give preference to the Divine Will and the happiness of his child over that of his personal joy. Far from opposing the celestial vocation, he had the courage to support it and he himself consecrated his daughter to the Lord. When he saw himself on the verge of death, he recommended the future orphan to his relative Elizabeth.

St. Anne, mother of Mary, loved her daughter with a tenderness that cannot be expressed. For her part, Mary takes pleasure in having her mother honoured. Her filial zeal is fully revealed in these words which she addressed to one of St. Anne's servants: 'I am your sister; and since you have always honoured my mother, I and my mother will close hell before you.'[6]

St. Joseph was of all men the one who most greatly loved the most Blessed Virgin. Who can tell of the sweet and pure affections exchanged between the heart of Joseph and the heart of Mary? Mary was the joy of Joseph, Joseph was the consolation of Mary. Joseph consecrated his life to support Mary and her Divine Son. Mary, helped by her Divine Son, supported Joseph at the time of death. What a beautiful life! What a sweet death!

ജ ❀ െ

---

6   I.e. this person was granted the grace of salvation and hell would be closed to them. Unfortunately, Fr. de Boylesve does not give more details on this private vision.

3. The Immaculate Conception

By an anticipated application of His merits, the Son of God preserves from original sin She who is to be His Mother. *There* is the One that was to crush the head of the serpent! Finally a daughter of Adam found favour with God; Mary is conceived without sin. From the first moment of her existence, She is the object of the blessings of the Heavenly Father who sees in Her His beloved Daughter, of the Son who contemplates in Her as a dear Mother, of the Holy Spirit who considers in Her His chaste and faithful Spouse.

For us, alas! We were born into disgrace before God; but a few hours after our birth, baptism delivered us from original sin. Where is the grace of innocence which had been so mercifully returned to us?

These words inspired by the Holy Spirit were addressed to Mary conceived without sin; 'You are all beautiful and no stain is in you,' *Tota pulchra es, and macula non is in te.* ("Thou art all fair, and there is not a spot in thee." Canticles. 4:7)

The words which the angel was to address later in the name of the Trinity of which he was the ambassador, had all their truth from the first moment of her existence; for from then on she was full of grace, from then on the Lord was with her, from then on she was blessed among all women and above all the daughters of Adam.

Preserved from all sin, full of grace from the first moment of her conception, Mary begins from then on to correspond with admirable fidelity to the graces of which God had preserved for her. In Mary, there is not a thought, not an intention, not an affection, not a desire, not a movement that is not of God and for God. This impulse of the Immaculate Virgin towards her God will continue to increase until her last breath. Who will be able to measure the height to which will rise this incomparable Virgin, so aptly named Mary, that is to say the Sovereign, the Most High?

If during the course of a single day we responded with constant fidelity to all the advances, all the inspirations of grace, what progress, what merit at the end of the day! And if the days and years followed one another in this way, at the end of our life what glory! Let us finally start, and do not say: 'It is too late'.

O Mary, conceived without sin, Immaculate Virgin, if you had to choose between the Divine Motherhood and preservation from original sin, you would not have hesitated. Rather than exist even for a single moment in the disgrace of God and under the empire of Satan, you would have renounced the honour of being the Mother of the Son of God made man. By this hatred[7] which you carry against Satan and sin, O Mary, Mother of Jesus and Our Mother, obtain for us the grace of fleeing sin as we would flee a serpent; have us die rather than ever committing a mortal sin. *Potius mori quam foedari.*[8]

But venial sin disposes and leads to mortal sin, it diminishes the action of grace in us, it disfigures the soul, it offends Divine Goodness; so obtain for us also

---

7   I.e. as in a 'holy hatred' for sin, a detestation of it.

8   The Latin phrase, "Better to die than to practise a foul act", or more popularly, "Death rather than dishonour." Of interest, this was also the motto of Brittany, that blessed region of France next to the Vendeé where Fr. Marin was from. These regions courageously fought against the Masonic-influenced French Revolution, defending both the Faith and the French Catholic Monarchy.

the grace to die rather than tarnish by the least sin the purity of our soul and our body.

The Relatives of Mary

St. Elizabeth was the first to salute the Mother of God, when enlightened by the Holy Spirit, she responded to the salutation of Mary with this cry of admiration: 'Blessed art thou among women, and blessed is the fruit of thy womb. And whence is this to me, that the Mother of my Lord should come to me? For behold as soon as the voice of thy salutation sounded in my ears, the infant in my womb leaped for joy. And blessed art thou that hast believed, because those things shall be accomplished that were spoken to thee by the Lord.'

St. John the Baptist leaped in his mother's womb at Mary's presence and was sanctified by this august visit. During his life he had frequent relations with Jesus and with the Blessed Mother, which contributed greatly to maintaining his affection for both. After his death he appeared more than once to the servants of Mary to excite them towards devotion to the Blessed Virgin. (*Nadasi.*)

St. Mary Salome, mother of the holy apostles James and John, was often found with the Most Holy Mother of Jesus of whom she was closely related. It was in her company that she drew this ardent love for the Saviour which inspired her with the courage to follow Him to Calvary and to stand at the foot of the cross. She buried the Body of Jesus and prepared the aromatics to anoint It.

The Birth of the Virgin

4. Her Nativity

It is said that the inventor of the game of chess asked for his wages a grain of wheat on the first square, two on the second, four on the third and so on, always doubling until the sixty-fourth. The request seemed modest. But the calculation being made, it turned out that all the wheat produced on the earth during a year would not have reached the proposed figure, and that all this wheat spread over the whole of France would have formed a layer whose thickness would exceed one meter.

Shall we apply this admirable progression to Mary? No, this example is still is too weak. Jesus Christ offers us another measure. The grain of wheat, says the Saviour, when it falls on good soil returns thirty, forty, a hundred to one. Now what earth was ever more fruitful than the heart of Mary? Suppose therefore that at the first instant of her existence, the first degree of grace conferred on the Immaculate Virgin was equal to the sum of the grace given to all the angels and to all the saints taken together; at the second instant by faithful correspondence, Mary increased this first grace a hundredfold; at the third instant, each of these hundred new degrees is in turn increased a hundredfold, and so on, so that soon all the figures are lacking to follow the progression.

Now, if it is true as very serious theologians assert that Mary had the use of reason from the first moment of her existence, who will be able to say how high she had already reached at the moment of her birth? It therefore seems to me I see the angels hurrying around the cradle of the blessed child; I seem to hear them cry out at the sight of this daughter of Adam whom grace already raises above all the celestial phalanges: What do you think this child will be? *Quis putas puer iste erit?*

On earth, however, the world ignores the birth of this extraordinary child. Only Joachim and Anne, and perhaps a few relatives, see future greatness. But from the height of Their throne the Three Divine Persons fix on her a look of benevolence: it is in the virginal womb of this child in which will be accomplished the reconciliation of earth and heaven, the irrevocable union between God and man, the mystery of the Incarnation.

The Apostles and Mary

St. Peter, Prince of the Apostles, during Mary's lifetime erected a chapel in her honour. He changed into a church the house where the Blessed Virgin had been born and received her first education. He always preserved the tenderest respect for the one who had obtained for him forgiveness for his triple renunciation.

St. Paul, Apostle of the Gentiles, inspired Thecla, his eldest daughter in the faith and the first martyr among women, with a fiery love for the Holy Virgin. Also, when the Mother of God appears to her servants, she is often accompanied by St. Thecla.

St. Andrew, Apostle, according to the testimony of St. Augustine had the honour to propose the article of the symbol expressed in these terms: *Born of the Virgin Mary.* On the day of the Mother of God's funeral, he spoke eloquently about her conception. From the height of the cross on which he consummated his martyrdom, he publicly taught that Mary had been conceived without sin. (*Bl. Amadeus.*)

ଌ ❀ ଔ

5. Noblesse Oblige

In remembrance of Mary's birth, remember yours, and thank God for the natural advantages you may have encountered when you entered this world, and above all for the rights of which the birth of the future Mother of the Saviour was the first origin. Alas! Whatever your condition in life is, you were born to suffer! Console yourself at the sight of the Immaculate Virgin. She is born free from sin, she is born full of grace, and yet she is born to suffer herself, as much and more than all mankind put together.

Remember also that nobility obliges, *noblesse oblige.* Your cradle, it is true, was not surrounded by grace and glory like that of the very pure and very holy Mother of God; however, you have received favours which distinguish you from the majority of men presently existing on the earth.

The population of the globe is estimated at fourteen hundred million. Of this number, there are barely four hundred million Christians: you were born among Christians. Of these four hundred million Christians, there are eighty million schismatics, almost as many heretics: you were born among the two hundred million Catholics.[+] Isn't this already a special grace, a grace which calls for your gratitude, a grace which calls for a faithful correspondence? - I cannot say anything about the graces which are personal to you and which only you know. For you, these are quite specific titles of greater and more singular fidelity.

These graces of which God preserved for you even before it was possible for you to deserve them, recall the mustard seed which must become a great tree; the seed sown in the ground which must produce thirty, sixty, a hundred to one; the talent that you must double with your work. What use have you made of your life, of intelligence, of freedom, of the senses? Ah! If since the moment when the eye of your reason opened, you had brought to God all your thoughts, all your words, all your actions, what treasures of grace amassed! What a crown of glory for all eternity! But unfortunately what graces were lost on the highway! How many good desires have remained ineffective like the stalk withered by the rays of the sun! So many resolutions stifled by temporal solicitations, like the seed enveloped in thorns. So many buried talents![**]

[+]   Note, Fr. De Boylesve was writing this for French-speaking Catholic readers that were born in predominately Catholic countries.

[**] I.e. a reference to the parable of the sower whose seed gets thrown onto various types of ground, from the hard pathway, to the rocky and thorny soil, and also the fertile soil. Also regarding the buried talents: a reference the parable of the servant given the one talent by his master, but did not increase

Do not say, however: 'It is too late'. The eleventh hour may have already struck for you when you have only a few years, a few days, a few hours left to live, yet you can make up for lost time; you may even by your fervour deserve a reward equal to that of the workers of the first hour.[+] Mary, by her example, will tell you how you should respond to the graces God has reserved for you. The fidelity of Mary manifests itself especially in three memorable circumstances: on the day of her Presentation, on the day of the Annunciation, and the day of the Purification.[#]

The Apostles and Mary (Continued)

St. James the Greater, close relative of Jesus and Mary, preached the Gospel in Spain and was visited by the Blessed Virgin who was still living on the earth. By her order he built a church in her honour which was for Spain the cradle of religion.[&]

St. Jude Thaddeus also had the significant

---

it, he buried it and handed it back as is, which angered the master. A symbol of the graces and talents God gives us.

[+]   I.e. a reference to the parable of the compassionate master of the vineyard who paid a full day's wages to those who were hired late to work.

[#]   Fr. de Boylesve seems to be saying here the examples shown by Our Lady in the Gospels at these events teaches us how to correspond with the graces given to us and thereby increase our graces like she did, also, he seems to say if you wish to ask for assistance from Our Lady, these feast days are particularly efficacious times to request graces from her.

[&]   The famous bi-location of the Blessed Virgin to St. James at the site that is now known as the shrine of Our Lady of Pillar in Spain.

honour of being a close relation to Jesus and Mary. He distinguished himself by his love for both. A glorious martyrdom crowned his life and his works for the propagation of the faith. He is invoked in all present necessities.

St. Bartholomew used to pray a hundred times at night and a hundred times during the day. The Mother of God, while still living on the earth, bestowed on him reported benefits. He had the good fortune to converse with her often and he learned from her a great number of heavenly mysteries. He propagated devotion to her in greater Armenia and in India. He ended up being flayed alive, and, by this brutal martyrdom, he merited to enter heaven.

ಬಿ ❀ ಚ

6. The Presentation

At the age of three years Mary was presented at the temple for her solemn consecration to God. By this consecration she sacrificed her family from whom she was separated, her person by her vow of virginity, and her liberty by the submissive and regulated life that she will lead in the temple.

Sacrifice of her family: sacrifice for the parents, sacrifice for the child.

Sacrifice for the parents: Joachim and Anne were advanced in age. Mary is the joy of their old years. But, recognizing that their child belongs to God before belonging to themselves, they resign themselves to a

separation which must have been so sensitive to them, and they offer to the Lord what they hold most dear.

Sacrifice for the child: Mary sees and feels the pain of her parents; and for her heart so tender and so loving this separation is no less painful for her than for them. She advances, however, she ascends the steps of the temple, she prostrates herself to accomplish her sacrifice.

Is God asking of you what is most dear to you? Resign yourself, rejoice. Resign yourself: God is the Master; all that you are, all that you have, it is from Him that you have it; He has the right to demand it, to ask for everything again. Rejoice when God asks for what is yours, when especially He asks for yourself, it is not for Him, He does not need you; it is for you, it is for your honour and for your happiness.

Sacrifice of her person by the vow of virginity. Anne and Joachim probably believed without doubt that their daughter's sacrifice extinguished their posterity. This is an error. This sacrifice ensures forever the kingship of the family, and that in an order and in a sense superior to anything they could conceive and desire.

Mary, on her part by her vow of virginity thought she had renounced the honour of motherhood. But by the grace of this vow, she will be the happiest and most glorious of mothers. God does not need our gifts or ourselves. When He asks of us, what we have and what we are, it is not to take them from us, it is to keep them for us, it is that He may give them back to us transformed, supernaturalized, deified. The glass of water that you gave to a poor person for the love of God turns for you into an eternal and infinite degree of glory. So it is with any action done in a state of grace and for God. Did I say, any action? God, who searches minds and hearts, takes into account our very thoughts and desires. In His eyes, intention includes the merit and value of execution. Man recognizes and rewards only effective service; God recognizes and rewards simple goodwill, even when strength has failed to achieve the desired good. Give therefore to God, give. His glory, in accordance with His goodness, forbids Him to let Himself be defeated in generosity. You give one thing, He will give back a thousand; you give an instant, He will give eternity; you give yourself entirely, He will give you Himself.

The Evangelists and Mary

St. Matthew, once a wealthy publican became zealous for the honour of the Blessed Virgin. (*Eusebius, Ecclesiastical History*)

St. Mark, Evangelist, had frequent talks with the Mother of God, and he learned many things from them which he reported in his Gospel. When the enemies of the faith sought him to put him to the torments, he saw his name written in heaven. (*Nicephorus; l. Ii, c. XLII.*)

St. Luke was a physician, a painter and Evangelist. Not content with writing about Mary in his Gospel, he painted several portraits of the Blessed Mother. These paintings, which have become famous for a large number of miracles, have greatly contributed to make her loved.

St. John was Evangelist, theologian, Apostle, prophet, virgin, and above all, he was the disciple whom Jesus loved, and, without a doubt, he was no less dear to Mary than to Jesus. He always had the most tender veneration for the Mother of God, but it was quite another thing when by the will of the dying Jesus he became the son of this dear Mother. From that moment, he did not cease to serve her with an entirely filial love during all the time that she lived on the earth.

ଔ ❀ ଔ

7. Her Life in the Temple

Mary sacrificed her liberty. In the temple, she lived a life of obedience. The rule seizes every moment, all the acts of her life. There is nothing to tell about the years that the Blessed Virgin passed in obscurity in the temple. To the eyes of man, all her actions seemed small and ordinary. But by doing well and for God alone what God wanted, the child grew in age, in grace and in wisdom, before God and before men, and without her knowing it became worthy of Divine Motherhood.

Following Mary's example, we presented ourselves to God on the day of our First Communion; every year we are invited to present ourselves to receive the Paschal Communion and this invitation is repeated to us at all feasts, or rather every day, because every day Jesus offers Himself to us and wants to give Himself to us, if every day we present ourselves to Him. - At least once a week we are ordered to present ourselves to attend Mass, and this invitation is repeated to us every day - every day also, and in the morning and in the evening, a holy custom urges us to present ourselves to

God through prayer.　Did I say, every day?　At every moment we can present ourselves to God, Who on His part is always present to us.　If He has given us intelligence it is to continually think of Him, if He has given us memory it is to constantly remind us of His presence; if He has given us free will it is to love Him and serve Him by the perpetual accomplishment of His Will.　It is up to us to live, like Mary, in the temple.　Is not the world around us a temple where everything manifests the presence, the power, the goodness, the wisdom of God Who has made everything and Who preserves and governs all things?

Retreat within yourself; God is present there, and by this light which enlightens every man coming into this world, and by this grace which gives you the right to be called His son and to be indeed: *Ut filii Dei nominemur et simus*, ("that we should be called, and should be the sons of God." 1 John 3:1), while awaiting for Him to show Himself face to face and as He is in Himself, and that by this sight He makes you like unto Him and that He permits you enter into His joy and His glory.[**]

The Holy Fathers and Mary

St. Denis,[+] roughly flogged then roasted on an

[**]　　A reflection based on 1 John, (3:2) "Dearly beloved, we are now the sons of God; and it hath not yet appeared what we shall be. We know, that, when He shall appear, we shall be like to Him: because we shall see Him as He is."

[+]　　　St. Denis of Paris (d. 250 AD).　According to the accounts of his martyrdom, he was forced to endure roasting on a grill, then abandoned to the ravages of wild animals, was afterwards thrown in a furnace, and then crucified, but all

iron bed, was assisted by Mary at the moment of his death. He had been fortunate enough to see her during his lifetime, and the sight made such an impression on him that, were it not for the teachings of the faith, he would have mistaken her for a goddess. (*Canisius*).

St. Basil the Great preserved his virginity through prayer, fasting, and study. This exquisite purity made him all-powerful over Mary's heart. One day, at the head of his people, he begged the Blessed Virgin to deliver the Church from the fury of Julian the Apostate, St. Mercury, whose relics were honoured in this place, let him know that he had been heard, and that at that very moment the Apostate had just been struck with death.

St. John Chrysostom defended the Divine Maternity of Mary against the Arians, St. Cyril saw him in heaven sitting beside Mary who, in turn, defended him against slander.

St. Cyril, Patriarch of Alexandria, presided over the Council of Ephesus and there zealously defended the Divine Motherhood of Mary against the impious Nestorius. It was he who, in this same council, added the words to the Angelic Salutation: 'Holy Mary, Mother of God, pray for us sinners, now and at the hour of our death.'

ഇ ❀ ര

---

these torments did not kill him due to his fervent prayers until he was finally beheaded. Another miracle occurred: he picked up his head and continued to preach, walking all the while from the site of Montmartre in Paris until he finally fell down dead to the north of the city where the church of St. Denis is located.

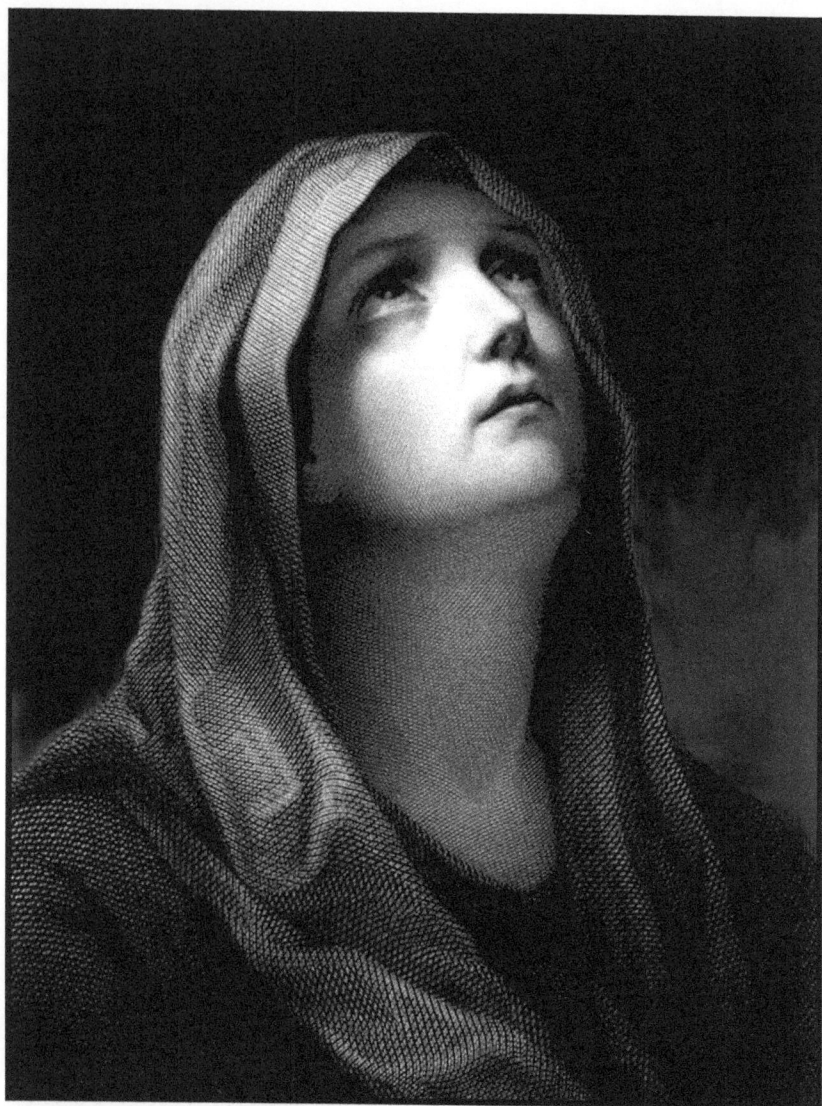

8. The Sigh of the Virgin

The night of error and of sin hangs over the world. A little longer and the people of Judah will merge into the pagan empire of Rome, and soon the true God will no longer have worshippers here below. Lucifer hovers over the nations as conqueror and master. The angels press around the foot of the Throne of the Divine Majesty, imploring for mankind a glance of pity - And God waits. - Suddenly, a sigh comes from the earth, crosses the heavens and rises even higher than the desires of the most ardent Seraphim.

From the depths of her unknown cell, a young girl of Judah implored the God of Abraham and David to hasten the coming of the Saviour promised for so many centuries. For herself, she begged the favour of being the humble servant of the Mother of this Son of Abraham in whom all nations were to be blessed, of this Son of David, whose reign was to extend over all centuries. - At this sigh, the Divine Justice lets Itself bend; the Three Persons said, 'Let Us bring about the redemption of the human race.'

Powerful and famous men seem to rule the world by words or by force; but there is a word, it is a more powerful action and which alone suffices to change the face of the world. This word, this action, is *prayer*.

At a sign from the Most High, St. Gabriel swiftly flew - Where is he going? - There is a point on the globe to which at that time all eyes were turned. This point is called Rome. Therein lies the centre of politics; there, they believe at least, the fate of nations is decided. - St. Gabriel has nothing to do in Rome. - Where is he going? - There is another point on earth which the intelligences of the elite are grouped around. This point is called Athens. There is the centre of wisdom. There from the height of their pulpits the philosophers give themselves out to be the kings of thought. - St. Gabriel has nothing to do in Athens. - Where is he going? - There is in the East a country despised by Athens and Rome. It is Judea. In this country there is a region despised even in Judea; it is called Galilee. In Galilee there is a city of which the proverb says: 'Can anything good come out of Nazareth?' In this city, in one of the humblest lodgings of this city, in a secluded cell, a virgin, daughter of David it is true, but poor and unknown, is at prayer. It is this prayer which has just crossed the heavens; and it was to answer this prayer that St. Gabriel, the ambassador of the Three Persons of the August Trinity, came down to earth. Enter the modest cell, bow down with the Archangel before the humble Daughter of Judah; listen.

Finally, let us understand that greatness is neither in Rome nor in Athens, that it is neither found in the power nor in the wisdom of the world. This virgin, unknown to the whole world, is however the greatest in the world. It is in obscurity, it is hidden in secret, it is in the depths of the soul that glory resides: *Gloria filiae regis ab intus.* ("All the glory of the king's daughter is within," Psalm 44: 14)

The Holy Fathers and Mary (Continued)

St. John of Damascus, from his earliest childhood, devoted himself to the service of Mary. Having had his right hand cut off because he had written in defence of holy images, the Mother of God restored it to him. Since then he ceased not to write in honour of Mary.

St. Ambrose drew an admirable portrait of Mary. He shows her to us keeping the most exact modesty: "Never," he adds, "was she less alone than when she was alone, always having for company the angels, her chaste thoughts and the holy scriptures."

St. Jerome defended the glory of Mary by his pen. His life was spent near the cave where the Blessed Virgin gave birth to Saviour. His body rests in the Church of Saint Mary Major. While living and also in death, his home is near Mary.

St. Augustine, after having groaned too long under the slavery of passion, surrendered his whole heart to virtue. His pen attests to his tenderness towards the Queen of Virgins. It is he who, with all the authority given by genius enlightened by faith, has declared that when there is a question of sin, there can be no question with regards to Mary in any way.[9]

80 ❀ 03

---

9   i.e. that she is and always was sinless. There is no question of it.

9. The Annunciation

Let us hear the words of the archangel. Ambassador of the Most High, he speaks on behalf of He Who sends him. It is therefore God Himself Who through the voice of St. Gabriel declares that Mary is full of grace, that He is with her and that she is blessed amongst all women.

Let us salute with respect the one whom God Himself has greeted by one of the seven angels in heaven who fulfil the function of assistants to the Throne of the Sovereign Majesty.

While the Virgin is astonished and humbled, the Archangel continues: 'You will have a son who is the Son of the Most High and Whose reign will be endless.'

O you who long for liberty, serve this King; the One that is there above you. Because if He is the Son of Mary, if He is a man like you, He is also the Son of God, He is God. Power and authority belong to Him alone, and only to those who represent Him here below and who command in His name. Long enough have you been the slave of your peers by your self-interest, by fear, by complacency, by human respect, often even of those who are not worthy of you by intelligence, by character, by dignity. Raise your forehead so as not to bow it any more, except before the Eternal King and His representatives: *et regni ejus non erit finis.* (And His kingdom shall have no end.)

St. Gabriel has fulfilled his mission, Heaven awaits the answer. - *Ecce ancilla Domini,* 'Behold', replies Mary, 'the handmaid of the Lord.' On behalf of God the angel proposes to her she would become the

Mother of the One who will be Great *par excellence* – *Hic erit magnus.* ('He shall be great and shall be called the Son of the most High', Luke 1:32) She declares herself the servant. In her mind this statement is not a simple formula. Such was always and such will be her condition, her state, her profession: to obey God, to serve God; and when she adds this word of consent to the word of the Divine messenger: *Fiat mihi secundum verbum tuum,* be it done to me according to thy word, she only expresses and repeats the sentiment and the habitual and constant resolution of her heart. Never has she desired and never will she desire anything but what God desires; always she wanted, and she will always want everything that God wants.

We are afraid of stooping down by obeying! We fear to degrade ourselves by serving! We fear dishonouring ourselves by humiliating ourselves! O madness and clumsiness of pride! Seek to raise yourself, and all will unite to lower you. Humble yourself, and every one will compete for the honour of exalting you. Humility is the sign, the hallmark of true greatness, the secret of true glory. But humility is shown above all through submission, which delights in obeying and serving. *Ecce ancilla Domini; fiat mihi secundu verbum tuum.* 'Behold the handmaid of the Lord, be it done unto me according to thy word.'

The Holy Fathers and Mary (Continued)

St. Peter Chrysologus, not content to inspire love towards the Most Blessed Virgin by his preaching, he defended the honour of the Mother of God with his writings against the heresy of Eutyches.

St. Leo the Great defended the dignity of Mary against the Nestorians, and he displayed the greatest activity to support the honour of the Mother of God, sending out everywhere decisive letters against the adversaries of the dogma of the Divine Maternity.

St. Gregory, pope, so great was his zeal for the honour of Mary above all the rest, seeing Rome desolate by a dreadful plague, had the image of the Blessed Virgin painted by St. Luke carried in procession. They then saw an angel put his word back in the scabbard, while other angels sang the *Regina Coeli.*[*]

ℰↄ ✤ ℭ

10. The *Fiat* of Mary

Admire the power of obedience; recognize the greatness and the glory in the same act of submission, and of a most profound humility. Standing as a servant and only wanting to be a servant, Mary replies to the angel: 'Fiat, let it be done unto me according to thy word.' At that instant the Father sent the Son; the Son abased and humbled Himself: *Humiliavit semetipsum* (Philp. 2: 8); He is annihilated, so to speak: *Semet ipsum exinanivit:* He takes the form of the slave, *formam servi accipiens*; He becomes Incarnate, He becomes a man like us, and by the operation of the

---

[*] The famous image of St. Michael appearing with Our Lady over Castel Sant'Angelo in Rome that announced the end of the deadly plague in the city, 590 AD,

Holy Spirit, He takes a body and a soul like us in the womb of the Immaculate Virgin. Thus the humble servant becomes the Mother of Him who is the Great One *par excellence*.

Mary said: 'Fiat'. At this word God operates His masterpiece, the Incarnation. There the Creator and the creature, Divine nature and human nature, God and man are united without being confounded, in the person of Jesus Christ, Son of God, Son of Man, Son of the Most High, Son of Mary.

Fiat: Let it be done unto me according to thy word. This word sums up the whole life, all the holiness, all the greatness of Mary. She never knew, never wanted to hear or do anything other than what God wanted her to be and to do.

Let us also say: *Fiat*; let God do what He wants with us. Let Him accomplish in us His word, His idea, all that He wants to do that is beautiful and great in us, and through us. Let us be under His gaze and in His hand, like the servant who awaits the master's order, like the instrument which receives all its movement from the hand of the artist; soon we will become a masterpiece and in our turn we will produce masterpieces. Like Mary, we will give life to Jesus, in ourselves first, then in others. It is Jesus Himself that declared: 'My mother and my brethren are they who hear the word of God, and do it.' *Mater mea and brothers mei hi sunt who verbum Dei audiunt and faciunt.* (Luke 8:21)

The Holy Fathers and Mary, (Continued)

St. Peter Damien left a number of writings in honour of Mary. By his care the daily recitation of the Office of the Blessed Virgin became a custom in several monasteries. He wanted to breathe his last in a convent dedicated to the Mother of God. His brother, named Marin, had drawn from his school such a zeal for the devotion of the Queen of Heaven that he put a rope around his neck, thus declaring himself the slave of the Holy Virgin. Every year he deposited on the altar of his Sovereign a sum of money as a tribute. (*Surius*.)

St. Anselm, Archbishop of Canterbury, left beautiful testimonies of his affection for Mary in numerous writings that he composed to her praise. He consecrated his virginity to her. To extend devotion to her, he erected churches and monasteries in her honour. Having fallen one night in a deep cistern, he was pulled out by Mary safe and sound. He ensured the feast of the Immaculate Conception of the Blessed Virgin was celebrated.

St. Bernard received such favours from Mary that he became like the foster brother of the Infant Jesus, since the Blessed Virgin gave him some of her own milk.** He kept these words on his lips all the

---

**   The famous miraculous "Lactation of St. Bernard". One day St. Bernard of Clairvaux was venerating an image of Our Lady holding the Christ child, and the statue of Our Lady exposed her breast and squirted some of her milk into his mouth as he was kneeling. Other accounts say it squirted into his eye and healed an infection, however, from that time on he became wise and eloquent, and would become the key

time: 'Hail, Mary; show that you are our Mother.' One day as he was reciting this in front of an image of Mary, he heard this response: 'Hail, Bernard'.

ഇ ❀ ര

11. The Ave Maria

Mary, Immaculate Virgin, Mother of Jesus and our Mother, with the Archangel Gabriel I too salute you: *Ave Maria*, Hail Mary. Thou art full of grace. In thee there was never room for the slightest sin; like the Ark of the Covenant, thou art entirely covered with the purist gold of charity, thou wert invested with it from the first moment of thy creation: *Gratia plena*, full of grace.

The Lord, the Sovereign Master, has always been with thee; but since thy response to the word of the angel, the Word became Incarnate in thy womb, the Saviour Jesus is in thee, and for thirty years He will be with thee, and today thou art with Him for all Eternity: *Dominus tecum*, the Lord is with thee.

Thou art blessed among all women. Eve was the mother of mankind according to nature, thou art Mother of mankind according to grace; Sarah was the mother of the son of the promise, thou art the Mother

---

reformer of the Cistercian order in the 12th century. In addition to his holiness, he was a gifted preacher and brilliant theologian. He was canonized 21 years after his death and in 1830 was officially honoured with the title of Doctor of the Church.

of Him in Whom is realized all promises; Deborah delivered the people of God, thou delivered all the peoples of the earth through thy Son; Jahel and Judith struck the enemy of Israel, thou crushed the head of the infernal serpent, the enemy of the entire human race; Esther diverted the wrath of Ahasuerus from Israel, thou dost divert the Divine wrath ready to break forth upon the whole world: *Benedicta tu in mulieribus*, blessed art thou among women.

The Fruit of thy womb is blessed. Thou art the Tree of Life, thou givest to the world the Fruit of True Life: intellectual life, for thy Son is Truth and Eternal Wisdom; supernatural life, for thy Son is the Principle of grace: *Benedictus fructus ventri tui Jesus*, Blessed is the fruit of thy womb, Jesus.

O Mary, holy and Immaculate Mother of God! Pray for us, poor sinners, for us although sinners, for us because we are sinners and as such we have a greater need of thy compassion: *Ora pro nobis peccatoribus*, Pray for us sinners.

Pray for us now: on this day, at this hour, at this moment when thy help is necessary for us, either to return to grace with Jesus, or to remain faithful to Him: *Nunc*, now.

Pray for us now, and may this 'now' last forever, may it continue until the hour of our death, until this decisive hour on which our eternity depends: *Et in hora mortis nostrae,* And at the hour of our death.

At this last hour come, O Mary, come and console me, come and relieve me, come and strengthen me, come and receive the last breath of thy child, and present me thyself before the Sovereign Judge who is also thy Son. So be it.

The Holy Fathers and Mary (Continued)

St. Thomas Aquinas while yet a small child found a paper on which was written the 'Hail Mary'. As they wanted to take it away from him, he put it in his mouth, and thus it was not difficult to discover what this treasure was to him, object of such deep affection. It was through the Immaculate Virgin, Mother of the Word Incarnate, that Thomas by the purity of his life and by the fullness of his doctrine, became the 'Angelic Doctor' and the 'Angel of the School'.

St. Bonaventure reveals his devotion to Mary through the psalter he composed in her honour. The Blessed Virgin herself advised a monk to read it. The seraphic doctor commented on the Gospel of St. Luke, because it expands more on the Mother of the Saviour than the other evangelists.

St. Francis de Sales recited the rosary every day. - The demon having persuaded him that he was damned, he prostrated himself before an image of Mary and addressed this prayer to the Mother of Mercy: 'If I must hate God during eternity, grant that at least I love Him during this lifetime.'* By this heroic act he recovered confidence and peace. The foundation of the Order of the Visitation is a perpetual monument of his devotion to the Blessed Virgin.

---

*   I.e. the saint was so afflicted with the temptation he was damned, he thought he was doomed to hate God in hell for all eternity as love does not exist there, but prayed to Our Lady for the grace to love God at least for the rest of his life before he was damned – this prayer immediately put the devil's temptations of despair to flight, and the saint recovered his inner peace.

St. Alphonsus di Liguori renouncing the world hung his sword on the altar of Our Lady of Mercy. He composed several works in honour of the Blessed Virgin. One day he was celebrating the praises of this Blessed Mother, he seemed enlightened by the radiance that an image of Mary projected onto his face.

ಐ ✤ ೞ

12. The Visitation

Having learned from the angel that her relative Elizabeth was going to become a mother, Mary went to her to congratulate her on this favour. Three virtues above all emerge in this circumstance.

Charity: Mary rejoices in the happiness of her relative, and with delicate attention she hastens to show her the part she takes in her joy.

Humility: Great as he must be, Elizabeth's son will only be the forerunner of Him of Whom Mary is the Mother; add that the miracle of motherhood united with virginity is superior to that of fertile sterility.[10] Yet, Mary never ceases to show her relative the marks of respect and the consideration due to her age.

---

10   I.e. the miracle that Our Lady became the Mother of God with her virginity perfectly left intact by the grace of God is greater than childless virginity, even of a consecrated person.

Modesty: Reserved and cautious, the Blessed Virgin only passes through the world, she flees the eyes of men and hastens to arrive at Elizabeth's, to live there for three months in retreat the same as in Nazareth.

Let us know how to reconcile the attraction of piety, recollection and union with God with the duties of charity towards our neighbour. However, in relationships imposed by decorum, let us avoid curiosity and vanity, let us not seek to see or be seen.

Let us not be held suspect on the question of the rights to thoughtfulness or presence. The honour due to God by us will not be compromised by humility. The Holy Spirit will know how to maintain our dignity. No sooner has Elizabeth heard the greeting of Mary than she feels her child move, and at this movement is enlightened by a Divine inspiration, she recognizes the action of Him that the Virgin bears in her womb: 'Blessed art thou among all women', she cries, 'and blessed is the fruit of thy womb. And from where does this favour come that the Mother of my Lord should come to me?'

Conceal your virtues and your merits; do not speak of the graces you have received, nor of your personal works: God is responsible for revealing what may interest His glory and yours. But even then and above all then, humble yourself, efface yourself and give God the honour which belongs only to Him.

Therefore, seeing her secret revealed by the Holy Spirit Himself, the humble Virgin returns to God all the glory and the wonders operated in her.

The Bishop-Saints and Mary

St. Ignatius, Bishop of Antioch and distinguished martyr, died in the time of the Blessed Virgin and was very devoted to her. He consulted her in his doubts, and, according to Metaphrastus, he wrote her several letters and received several replies.

St. Nicholas is to be counted among the most ardent servants of Mary. He resisted with all his might the heretics who challenged the purity of the Immaculate Virgin. His zeal even brought him disgrace. He was dispossessed of his episcopal see. But Mary visited him and had him restored to his dignity. (*Lipomanus.*)

St. Martin, Bishop of Tours, was a model of all virtues, and especially of devotion to Mary whom he always honoured with a piety as solid as it was constant. In return he received reported favours from the Mother of God, and it is believed that it was through her protection at the point of death that he won a resounding victory over the demon. (*Sulpice Sévére*)

St. Boniface, apostle of Germany, after having converted the inhabitants of Thuringia, raised a church in honour of the Blessed Virgin to support the new Christians in the faith. Often he replaced their idols with the images of Mary, teaching that if God alone is to be worshipped, it is just to venerate her whom God Himself honoured to the point of choosing to be the Mother of the Word Incarnate. (Nadasi, *Année céleste.*)

හ❀ඏ

13. The Magnificat

Magnificat anima mea Dominum. "My soul glorifies the Lord." *Magnificat*, magnify. And who can *magnify* the Lord, who can add to His greatness? Whether He is known or not, praised or not, He will be neither more nor less great in Himself. Nothing could be more true. However we can magnify Him or make Him magnified in ourselves and in others. God magnifies in us when by study, by contemplation, we know Him and love Him more and more; we make Him magnified in others when we make Him known and loved. Now, no one knew God better, no one loved Him more, no one contributed more to making Him known and loved than the one who gave the world the Incarnate Word: "My soul glorifies the Lord," *Magnificat anima mea Dominum.* It is true that in speaking thus Mary only thinks of returning to God the honour of the great things accomplished in her, but by this very humility, she gives Him all the glory that she has received from Him.

Et exultavit spiritus meus in Deo salutari meo. "And my spirit rejoiced". It is by the spirit, by that which is purer, freer, the most elevated above the senses, the most disengaged from matter, that advances the soul. Who could follow the advancement of the immaculate soul of the Virgin Mary?

In Deo salutari meo. "In God my Saviour". In God alone is salvation: salvation of intelligence – for outside God all is darkness; salvation of the will – for outside of God all is powerlessness and base servitude. But united to God by placing faith in His word, I become wise by His very wisdom: united to God by charity, I become good by His goodness. By faith I think as He thinks, I speak as He speaks; out of charity, I want what He wants, I love what He loves.

Quia respexit. "Because He regarded", looked upon. The Divine glance lifts up and saves. Jesus looked at Simon: *intuitus eum.* ("looking on him") This gaze is his vocation to the apostolate. Simon has succumbed, Jesus looks at him: *respexit Petrum.*[+]

[+]   I.e. at his denial of Christ – the glance of the Lord brings him to repentance. "And the Lord turning looked on Peter. And Peter remembered the word of the Lord, as he had

This gaze lifts him up. - Now what attracts the Divine regard is humility.

Respexit humilitatem. "Because he hath regarded the humility ... ." On Mary's lips, here, humility means baseness. But the admission of baseness is already humility.

Humilitatem ancillae sua. "... the humility of His handmaid." Humility in thought and feeling is certainly a great and beautiful virtue. But in feeling and even in thought we can delude ourselves. We recognize its baseness, we feel its misery when it comes to putting oneself in the lowest rank – pride awakens and revolts. We thought pride was dead, it was only asleep. Real, complete, practical humility consists in submission, in obedience; it consists above all in serving. Mary declares that she is the servant: *humilitatem ancillae*; it is her profession, her condition, let us add that this profession is also her glory and her happiness.

Ecce enim ex hoc beatam dicent omnes generationes. "For behold, because of this, all generations will call me blessed." - Why? Because she is the mother of God? – No. Later, a woman addressing Jesus will cry out: 'Blessed is the womb that bore you!' Jesus will answer her, 'Say rather: Blessed are those who hear the word of God and keep it!' The happiness of Mary is therefore to have listened to the word of God which was transmitted to her by the Archangel, and to have submitted to this word, to have declared herself the servant, ready to obey and to want all that God would want. *Ecce ancilla Domini: fiat mihi secundum verbum tuum.* "Behold the handmaid

---

said: Before the cock crow, thou shalt deny me thrice. And Peter going out, wept bitterly." (Luke 22: 61-62)

of the Lord, be it done unto me according to thy word." This is the reason for Mary's happiness, she recognizes it: *Respexit humilitatem ancillae suae, ecc..* "Because he hath regarded the humility of his handmaid", etc. Because of this. – Because of the Divine glance if you prefer; but what sight attracted Him? The recognized and avowed baseness, the humility, the submission, the obedience of the servant: *humilitatem ancillae.* From there, *ex hoc,* the happiness of Mary; hence also her glory. Glory is to be known and praised. It is all the greater as it is more universal in terms of the number of people who know and who pay it due. Now, the happiness of Mary will be known and praised by all generations: *Beatam dicent me omnes generationes.* "For behold from henceforth all generations shall call me blessed."

Glory and happiness, however, cannot consist only in baseness, in humility, in submission. No, this state is only the foundation, *ex hoc,* the condition of glory and happiness. But given a humble and submissive heart, God is watching; and finding in that heart no obstacle to His designs, He does great things: *Quia fecit mihi magna qui potens est.* "Because He that is mighty, hath done great things to me." These great things, in Mary what are they? In Mary the Word was Incarnated, in Mary the Saviour was given to the world. These great things required nothing less than the Divine omnipotence: *fecit mihi magna qui potens est.* "He that is mighty, hath done great things to me."

The Bishop-Saints and Mary (Continued)

St. Thomas, Archbishop of Canterbury, while still young received from the Mother of God a casket containing a chasuble. Another time, Mary helped him mend a hair shirt worn out by long service. Every day the saint used to honour the seven joys of the Blessed Virgin when she was on earth. She urged him to also honour the joys she tastes in heaven, and promised to protect those who would pay her this homage. (See the Appendix regarding this devotion attributed to St. Thomas.)

St. Antoninus, zealous defender of the honour of Mary, prosecuted a heretic according to the law who had blasphemed against the Mother of God. She appeared to him at the moment of death, and after he greeted her with these words: 'Holy and immaculate virgin, I do not know by what praises with which to celebrate you,' he expired. (*Nadasi.*)

St. Charles Borromeo had an image of the Blessed Virgin placed at the door of all churches, and he advised all his diocesans to carry one with them. He ordered the canons to bow their heads at the name of Mary. Every day he recited the office of the Mother of God on his knees and he fasted on bread and water on the eve of her feasts.

ഹ ✿ രു

14. The Magnificat (Continued)

Et sanctum nomen ejus. ("And holy is His Name.") This great thing called the Incarnation declares the holiness of the Name of God. Holiness is the reunion of all perfection in God, the eternal union between the Three Divine Persons in the perfect unity of the same nature, the irrevocable union between God and man. It is this last union that the Incarnation achieves. In Jesus Christ our nature is irreversibly united with the Divine Nature. *Et sanctum nomen ejus.* "And holy is His Name". The angel said: *Quod nascetur ex te sanctum.* ("... the Holy which shall be born of thee." Luke 1:35)

And All Holy as He is, His goodness supports us. His holiness cannot suffer the slightest imperfection; but His mercy forgives he who fears to offend Him. *Et misericordia ejus a progenie in progenies timentibus eum.* ("And His Mercy is from generation unto generations, to them that fear Him.") But woe to the great ones, woe to those who in their hearts plan projects against God! The All Powerful will reach out and disperse the rebels. *Fecit potentiam in brachio suo; dispersit superbos mente cordis sui.* ("He hath showed might in His arm: He hath scattered the proud in the conceit of their heart.")

God gives power only for the salvation of the world; the powerful have stopped within themselves, they are seated in their pride: God puts them down and lowers them to the ground; then He replaces them with men that are nothing, by men who understand and recognize their nothingness. *Deposuit potentes de sede; et exaltavit humiles.* ("He hath put down the mighty from their seat, and hath exalted the humble.")

Happy are those who are weak and thirst for righteousness! They shall be filled. *Esurientes implevit bonis.* ("He hath filled the hungry with good things"). But those who believe themselves rich, who pass for such, and who are only so with earthly goods, only with honours, only with pride, these will be dismissed with empty hands and hearts. No one is more useless in the world than a rich man who, thinking only of enjoyment, forgets the poor and Divine worship; no one is also more unhappy. One cannot speak of the weariness, the desolation which egoistic enjoyment spreads in a heart: *Et divites dimisit inanes.* ("And the rich He hath sent empty away.") Far different from the powerful and the rich are God's people when compared to other peoples, they appear small and miserable. The other peoples are 'giants'; to them Israel is only a child: but God took him in His arms, He carries Him on His Heart: *Suscepit Israel puerum suum.* ("He hath received Israel His servant.") However guilty he (Israel) may have been, as soon as he repents, God forgets the threats of His justice, to remember only the promises of His mercy: *Recordatus misericordiae suae.* ("... being mindful of His mercy.")

He had promised the patriarchs a Saviour from their blood; He had declared to Abraham that in him and in his race, in the person of one of his sons that all the nations would be blessed, and that this son of blessing would be the King of Ages! This promise has just been fulfilled in the womb of Mary, daughter of Abraham, in the Person of the Word Incarnate, Son of God through His Eternal Generation, son of Abraham through his temporal generation. *Sicut locutus est ad patres nostros. Abraham and semini ejus in saecula.* ("As He spoke to our fathers, to Abraham and to his seed for ever.")

The Founders of Orders and Mary

Saint Benedict, father of an infinite number of monks, carried with him the relics of the Blessed Virgin with great respect. He wanted that in every church of his order there should always be a chapel consecrated to the Mother of God.

St. Bruno was so struck by the terrifying death of a doctor of Paris[11] and the judgement of God on this unfortunate man, that he retired to the desert where he founded the Order of the Carthusians. Mary promised the new institution her perpetual protection, on condition that the religious recite her office[12] everyday. She herself deigned to encourage the children of St. Bruno to observe a severe and rigorous discipline.

St. Norbert, bishop of Magdebourge, first stood out at court for the vanity of his conduct, but being

---

11   The doctor was Raymond Diocrès who died in 1084. He was a professor of the University of Paris and enjoyed a reputation for sanctity. Many assumed he would be a saint, but after his death his body briefly retuned to life during his funeral, and sitting up on his funeral bier he declared God had accused him, judged him, and he was condemned to Hell. St. Bruno was one of his students and witnessed this startling miracle. This made him reflect upon the vanity of a worldly career. He converted and founded the Carthusian order.

12   No doubt the 'Little Office of the Blessed Virgin' is meant here.

converted, he embraced a very austere life and founded the Order of Prémontré.[13] Mary gave him a white coat, a symbol of purity. When he died, his soul was seen carried to heaven in the form of a lily.

ℬ❀ℭ

15. <u>Nazareth and Bethlehem</u>

Mary remained three months with her venerable relative: then she returned to Nazareth to wait in silence and in obscurity for the birth of her Divine Son. She knew, however, from the prophecies of which she had perfect understanding, that the Saviour was to be born in Bethlehem. She relies on the Providence of a God, Who in order to accomplish His designs, will overthrow heaven and earth if necessary. Indeed, Augustus ordered the numbering of the subjects of the empire. By that, without seeing it, he ensured the fulfilment of the Divine oracles. Jesus is born in Bethlehem in an abandoned stable. Mary wraps Him in swaddling clothes and puts Him to bed in a manger.

Announced by the angels, the shepherds come to worship the Infant God: announced by a star, the kings come to offer Him their homage, and by symbolic gifts they recognize His royalty, His humanity, and His Divinity. In the presence of a Saviour Who has just been born, Mary disappears; all eyes, all hearts are

---

13   The Premonstratensians or Norbertines, they are also known as the White Canons in the UK and Ireland.

turned to the Divine Infant. After this point, the Mother will reappear only for the trial and the sacrifice.

The Founders of Orders and Mary (Continued)

Saint Jean de Matha, founder of the Order of the Trinity for the ransom of captives, found himself one day in a great embarrassment. He lacked the money needed for the ransom of one hundred and thirty slaves. Then kneeling before an image of the Blessed Virgin that he constantly wore on his heart, he revealed his distress to her. He immediately received from Mary the sum demanded for the redemption of these unfortunates. (*Lopez, Chronicle of the Order.*)

St. Francis of Assisi always wore an image of Mary on his heart. He was preparing for the Feast of the Assumption by fasting for forty days. Praying in the church of Portiuncula, he saw Mary asking Jesus for a special blessing and a plenary indulgence for those who would visit this church.[14]

---

14   In the beginning, this Indulgence was only available at the Portiuncula shrine, but was later extend to all churches and chapels of the Franciscans, and any order related to the Franciscans, such as the Carthusians, etc., or if there is no Franciscan or related order in any area, the local ordinary can designate a place to gain the Indulgence. How to gain the Portiuncula Indulgence: one must visit a Franciscan order church, chapel or specially designated chapel or oratory on August 2. To go to confession and receive holy communion, to pray for the intention of the Holy Father, and say the Our Father and the Creed. The Indulgence is Plenary if the person has no attachment at all to all venial sin, or, the Indulgence is Partial if there is any attachment to any venial sin.

St. Dominic, founder of the order of the Friar Preachers, obtained from Mary everything that he asked of her. As soon as he knew how to walk, he began to visit the churches that were dedicated to her. His most constant concern was to find new ways of honouring her. – It was he who spread the Holy Rosary everywhere. He once saw the Blessed Mother praying for the world that was to perish. At the time of his death he was conducted to heaven by Mary herself.

ကာ ✿ ဢ

16. The Purification

Joseph and Mary went up to the temple for the ceremony of the Purification. How many people will have seen Mary pass by and will have taken her for any mother like the others! How many will have seen Jesus in the arms of Mary or Joseph and will have looked at Him like any ordinary child!

You who are not greater than another, you who are quite ordinary, why do you want to be noticed, to be distinguished from the crowd?

Fix your gaze upon the two main characters of this mystery, on Jesus and on Mary, and consider those who intervene and who are referred to more specifically in the Gospel.

First of all St. Joseph, see how he fades away! – Accompany Jesus and Mary; serve them, but without being seen, and do not seek anything but that you may be forgotten.

There is the elder Simeon, who for so long awaited the happy day when he would be given the chance to see the Saviour with his own eyes. – Desire, ask, persist and do not despair. Your consistency will be rewarded.

There is Anne the prophetess, whose life is spent in prayer and fasting. – To persevering prayer, add continuous mortification, and the hour of consolation will come.

Finally, although the Gospel does not say it, the angels escort the Child and Mother, the Heavenly Father contemplates in this Child His beloved Son, and in the person of this modest Virgin who in the eyes of men passes for any mother similar to all others, He recognizes the Mother of the Incarnate Word.

Is it not enough for you to be seen and praised by God and the angels? The judgement and the esteem of heaven is not sufficient enough to console you for the contempt and forgetfulness of the earth?

Mary presents Jesus in the Temple. The elder Simeon receives Him in his arms. This Child, he says, will be the ruin and the resurrection of many.

Woe therefore to those who will oppose this Child and who would claim to prevent Him from growing in this Mystical Body that is also His Body and which is called the Church! Their opposition will pile up ruins; but it will not be the Church that will collapse.

Happy are those who take the Child in their arms for His Mystical Body, for His Church![15] Perhaps they will succumb in the fray, but they will rise up immortal and glorious.

This Child, continues the old man, will be a sign of contradiction. Do you yearn for the honour of serving God and saving souls? Expect contradiction: contradiction on the part of those who have an interest in ignoring the rights of God and losing souls in order to satisfy their passions; contradiction on the part of those very same ones whom you want to save, because in order to save them you are obliged to also contradict their prejudices and their passions.

Mary heard it all, she understood it all. There was no need for the prophet to add: "And you, a sword of sorrow will pierce your soul." Here we shall stop and consider the most Blessed Virgin.

The law of purification did not apply to Mary. Preserved from all sin, even from original sin, becoming Mother by the sole operation of the Holy Spirit, Mother of Him Who is Holiness itself: *Quod nascetur ex te sanctum;* ("the Holy which shall be born of thee", Luke 1:35) of Him Who by His very presence sanctified John the Baptist, Mary could not be purified. However, she submits to a law that does not concern her. Virgin afterwards as before childbirth, she presents her Divine Son, and by confusing herself with other mothers, she confuses her Son with ordinary children.[16] However, for Mary and for Jesus the

---

15   Fr de Boylesve also seems to say, blessed are they who accept Christ and His Church as easily as Simeon did accepting Him in his arms, and, who will defend His Church against its enemies.   These are the ones whom Simeon foretold will be resurrected.

16   'Confuse', meaning to mix up with as to be considered as or mistaken as something else.   Here Fr. de Boylesve is

fulfilment of this law will not be as for other mothers and for other children, a simple ceremony.

The offering is accepted. The Child is returned to the Mother, but He will be claimed when the hour of immolation has sounded. Also at this moment begins the sacrifice that must be consumed on the cross, here for Mary begins the series of sorrows already foreseen and accepted in the day and hour of *"Fiat mihi secundum verbum tuum."* ("Let it be done unto me according to thy word.")

The Founders of Orders and Mary (Continued)

St. Peter Nolasque (Nolasco) founded a religious order under the title Our Lady of Mercy for the redemption of captives by the command of the Blessed Virgin, together with the help of St. Raymond de Penafort, who had also received an announcement from Mary herself, and James King of Aragon. One night he saw Mary visiting the cells of her convent and protecting the religious during their sleep. Another time, as he was worried because of the distress of his house, the Blessed Virgin reassured him with these words: 'Do not be afraid, my son, I will not abandon you in your poverty. Just think of serving my Son and myself.' Having to preach and his voice failing, Mary restored it to full use. (Nadasi, *Celestial Year.*)

---

saying Our Lady mixed among the mothers and their children that day in the Temple and did not stand out, she and Jesus appeared no different than them and therefore were mistaken to be 'ordinary' just like everyone else.

St. Raymond de Penafort drew from the love of the Blessed Virgin as if it were milk.[17] The divine Mother ordered him to assist St. Peter Nolasque in the founding of the order of Our Lady of Mercy. Full of confidence in Mary, he sailed a hundred and sixty miles at sea without any other ship than his cloak. (Bzovinus, *Annales*.)[18]

St. Francis of Paolo from the age of thirteen until his death did not miss a single day of reciting the Rosary. He had in his cell an image of Mary that he often venerated. Louis XI, King of France, having wanted to replace this image by a painting of great

---

17   I.e. as a a little infant whose sole nourishment is its mother's milk, he spiritually lived on his love of Our Lady.

18   The story of this miracle: the saint was confessor to King James I of Aragon. Although the King was a devout man, he lived a sinful life in that he had a mistress. St. Raymond constantly told the King to give up his sinful life, but he refused to do so. Then, St. Raymond was brought by the King to the island of Majorca to propagate the faith among the people there who were mostly Moors. The King also arrived on the island, and, he brought his mistress. St. Raymond finally rebuked the King and asked him to dismiss her. When the King refused to send her away, the saint asked permission to leave the island. The King was furious and refused permission, also declaring the death penalty for anyone who attempted to help the saint to leave the island. St. Raymond responded: "An earthly king withholds the means of flight, but the King of Heaven will supply them."

Walking to the seashore, he removed his cloak and spread it upon the water. He tied up one corner of it to a staff for a sail, and having made the Sign of the Cross, stepped upon it confidently and set off. There were many boats and other sailors at sea who watched in astonishment as he sailed by. In six hours he crossed 160 miles and reached the harbour of Barcelona! The miracle was witnessed by thousands. On arriving at the harbour he gathered his cloak which was miraculously dry. The King repented and gave up his sinful life.

price, the saint refused to do so.[19] It was to Mary that Francis attributed the glory of miracles that he operated in such large numbers.[20]

ഇ ✿ beta

17. The First Sorrow – The Sword

At the announcement of the contradictions that await the Divine Child, the sword started to penetrate the heart of Mary. Until the moment when it will pierce it right through, this sword will sink every day into her maternal heart. Jesus grows in grace and wisdom before God and before men, every day He shows Himself more lovable, and every day Mary loves Him more. But what joy can a mother taste who knows that her dear Son, her only child, is destined for the most dreadful torture? The more she loves, the more she suffers.

---

19   Not that he was rejecting a picture of Mary, but in his humility and poverty he refused it as the new picture would have been rich and costly.

20   St. Francis of Paola is also called the 'Wonder-worker' – he too like St. Raymond of Penafort set sail across the ocean on his cloak, from Italy to France when the King France desired to see him but the boatmen refused him passage. There are so many miracles attributed to him, they even extend to animals - one day some hungry men had roasted and eaten a lamb the Saint looked upon as a pet: when he could not find the lamb, the men told them what happened. St. Francis looked at the bones in the fire and called into the ashes – the lamb playfully jumped out as if nothing had happened.

When she contemplates that beautiful brow, she sees it crowned with thorns; when she admires that gentle face, she sees it disfigured by cruel blows and soiled by vile spittle; when she feels the embrace of these little hands, she sees them pierced by nails; when she kisses those little feet, she sees them nailed to the cross. So do not think that Mary's life was spent in the sweetness of retreat with her Jesus, and that for her the pain did not begin until Calvary. As well as Jesus, Mary remained thirty-three years in front of the cross; since the prediction of Simeon, or rather since the announcement of the Divine Motherhood, the cross was always presented to her memory and to her heart: in her memory, she knew through the prophets what Christ was to suffer; to her heart, this Christ is her Son, her Jesus.

Let us beware of certain impulses which convince us that we are ready for anything for the glory of God, while in fact the slightest contradiction revolts us or overthrows us.

Often in offering ourselves to God we keep a secret deep desire that the offering will not be accepted, and a hidden hope that it will not be required.

The test will reveal the sincerity of our feelings and our words.

And so, as Simeon predicted, the calm resignation and the invincible constancy of our Mother reveals to us the thoughts and feelings of the most generous and greatest soul that has ever been after that of Jesus. It is for the glory of God, it is for our salvation that Mary endured this long martyrdom. See how much she loved God! See how much she loved us!

He who wants something suffers everything rather than give up his plan. And me, when it comes to the interests of God, of the honour of Jesus Christ, the defence of the Church, the salvation of souls, of my own perfection, the slightest suffering makes all my resolve vanish. It is not that I do not want to; it is that I do not understand what God is worth, what Jesus Christ is worth, what the Church is worth, what a soul is worth, what a degree of grace, of virtue, and of eternal glory is worth. However, for you and for Mary, the future is even darker than the present, and the present trials are only a preparation for future trials. Rest assured, however. Accept the cross of each day, and when the hour of the great sacrifice sounds you will be ready, if necessary you will be a hero, you will be a martyr.

The Founders of Orders and Mary
(Continued)

St. Ignatius of Loyola, after just converting, declared himself a knight of Mary and defender of her glory. After his vigil of arms in front of the altar of the Queen of Heaven in Mont-Serrat, he hung his sword there as a sign of his commitment to serve. He was often favoured by her visits. It was under her inspiration that he wrote the admirable book of the *Spiritual Exercises* and the *Constitutions of the Company of Jesus*. It was on the day of the Assumption that in Montmartre he made his vows with his first companions. He always carried with him the

image of the Immaculate Heart of Mary.

St. Philippe Neri put all his hope in Mary. Often he received visits from her, and through her he recovered his health. A beam in the oratory in which he prayed was once on the point of collapsing, he saw it supported by Mary. He used the image of the Mother of God as a seal.

St. John of God one day recited the *Salve Regina* before an image of the Blessed Virgin that was veiled. When he came to the words: 'Turn then ... thine eyes of mercy towards us', the veil was drawn back and Mary looked upon him. This tender Mother preserved him from many dangers, once when he was going to fall from a precipice, another time from the traps that the demon set for him. She even took the solicitude to wipe the sweat from his forehead as he worked.

ଛୁ ❀ ଓଃ

18. The Second Sorrow - The Flight into Egypt

What agonies, what apprehensions at the news that the life of the Divine Child is threatened by Herod! Who will tell of the difficulties, the solicitudes, the unavoidable privations of a flight made in haste?

At the same time, what a test for faith! What! This Child is the All Powerful God, the Master of Kings, and to escape the tyrant He has no other resource than flight! He is the Saviour of the World and He Himself must be saved by a poor craftsman and by a weak woman! Could He not have lost His enemy, or at least escaped His hatred by a less humiliating and less painful process? Mary worshipped in silence and her faith was not shaken for a moment.

With one breath Jesus could dispel the enemies of His Church; with a word He could calm the flood-tides that threaten her; with a look He could bring down all the obstacles that oppose the designs you have formed for His glory: but He wants to test your fidelity, your constancy and your humility. Flee with Him, withdraw, give in to the storm, suspend your work, your businesses. Herod will pass, the obstacle will fall and you will resume the work of God.

With the flight to Egypt there is connected a pain which was very sensitive to the heart of Mary. Far from the temple of the true God, the Holy Family sees itself transported into the midst of false divinities. Who can say how much the Heart of the Mother suffered for the sorrow felt by the Heart of the Divine Child reduced to living in the empire of Satan?

Obliged to live in a world which has forgotten the true God little less than the Egyptians of old, are we grieved by this spectacle? Do we regard this land as a land of exile? Alas! Too often the riches, the pleasures, the honours, all these idols which make up the unique religion of the children of the century,[21] charm us much more than the poverty, the sufferings, the humiliation of Jesus, and the false joys of the senses affect us more than the sorrow of our Mother.

---

21   'Children of the Century', or 'child of the age', i.e. an expression meaning those who live their lives by the worldly fashions and the 'progressive' knowledge, values or morals of the times.

The Religious Saints and Mary

Bl. Simon Stock had a tender devotion towards the Mother of God. One day when he was praying to her for sinners, she appeared to him holding the Carmelite (Brown) scapular in her hands, and she said to him: 'Receive this scapular; whoever dies wearing this habit will not suffer eternal fire.' Mary also promised to hasten the end of the sentences of Purgatory for her clients. (*Nadasi*). (See the Appendix for information on the Brown Scapular.)

St. Vincent Ferrier, while yet young, recited the office of the Blessed Virgin every day. He began all his sermons with the Angelic Salutation. (The Hail Mary). He advised the faithful to recite this beautiful prayer frequently.

Bl. Hermann, having asked the Blessed Virgin for health, was asked to choose between health and wisdom. He preferred wisdom, and suddenly he possessed all the sciences and all languages. The *Salve Regina (Hail Holy Queen),* and the *Alma Redemptoris* are his compositions.

฿ ❀ ๏

19. The Third Sorrow –
The Loss of the Child Jesus

Mary and Joseph were returning from Jerusalem, Mary without doubt with the holy women of her kinship, Joseph with the men. Mary thought that the Child Jesus, then aged twelve, had followed His adoptive father. Joseph assumed that the Child was with His Mother. What was not the surprise and the anguish of the one and the other when meeting again in the evening they discovered that the Child Jesus was neither with one nor with the other!

Consider the activity, the solicitude of their searches and yet the calm and the serenity which they retain in their affliction. If you want to get an idea of the sorrow of the Mother and of the adoptive father, listen to the sweet complaint that escapes from the lips and the Heart of Mary, when, after three days of anxiety, they finally find the Divine Child sitting in the temple among the doctors. 'My son', she said to Him, 'why hast thou done so to us? Behold thy father and I have sought thee sorrowing.' *Fili, quid fecisti nobis sic? Ecce pater tuus et ego dolentes quaerebamus te.*

O you who have the misfortune of losing Jesus by your fault, by mortal sin perhaps, when returning to yourself and you recognize the sad state of your soul, are you seized with sorrow as were Mary and Joseph who, however, had no fault to blame in the loss of the Divine Child? Is your first concern then to seek the grace and friendship of Jesus and to bring Him back to your heart by contrition and by confession?

Or when, if you have not driven Jesus from your soul by mortal sin, you have lost the fervour of devotion or the feeling of His presence as a result of your negligence in spiritual exercises and the lukewarmness of your life, do you have recourse to prayer, to the temple, to the Most Blessed Sacrament, to draw therein those Divine lights, those holy ardours without which you are ordinarily so blind and so cowardly in the service of God?

The Religious Saints and Mary (Continued)

Bl. Albert the Great, who was the master of the Angelic Doctor,[22] did not naturally receive great faculties. Discouraged at seeing so little capacity for study, he thought of leaving the religious profession. But the Mother of God prevented him and obtained for him such prodigious dispositions for science that he acquired immortal glory in this genre. Also Albert could not hear pronounced the holy name of Mary without bursting into tears.

St. Anthony of Padua learned from Mary herself that the hymn *O gloriosa Domina* was very agreeable to her, and he died reciting it. [++] (See the Appendix for

---

22   i.e. a master of St Thomas Aquinas.

[++] NOTE: Fr. De Boylesve may have unintentionally mixed two traditions together here.   One says it was another monk in Portugal to whom Our Lady revealed that this hymn pleased her the most. The other relates St. Anthony heard this hymn sung by his mother when he was yet a little child, it became his favourite hymn, and he sang it on his

the Hymn.) Finding himself outside in a rainy day, he put his rosary on his head and did not receive a drop of water. The demon wanted to strangle him one day, but in the name of Mary he fled. This Blessed Mother assisted him during his last breath.

St. Bernadine of Siena was very devoted to the images of Mary. One day he was reciting the Rosary on his bare knees and with great attention, the Blessed Virgin deigned to appear to him and speak to him thus: 'Bernadine, my faithful servant, your devotion pleases me very much.' As he preached the praises of the Mother of God, a star was seen shining over his head. The same prodigy was renewed above his body after his death. (*Chronicle of the Friars Minors.*)

℠❀℣

20. The Fourth Sorrow – The Meeting

Thirty years pass in the obscurity of Nazareth, but in stillness and peace. Then for three years Mary, with joy mingled with the most saddest presentiments, follows the preaching of her Divine Son. She rejoices at the influx of people who, attracted by His miracles, crowd around Him to hear Him. But the murmurs of the Pharisees and their threats only give a glimpse of the outcome.

---

deathbed. See the Appendix to learn of the miraculous appearance of Our Lady to the monk in Portugal.

Finally the hour of darkness has come, Jesus is arrested. Condemned by the high priest, scourged, crowned with thorns, abandoned by Pilate, charged with the cross to which He will be nailed, He climbs Calvary.

Most of the time the imagination exaggerates the evils it foresees. It is rare this reality[23] is not underneath our fears and our forebodings. For Mary it is quite different. Enlightened by the prophecies of which she had such a perfect understanding, she had imagined the Passion of her Son under the most painful features. But its accomplishment exceeds our forecasts.

Look at Jesus torn apart by the scourging, covered in His own Blood which flows from all His Wounds. From head to toe, His Body is a wound. Look at this crown, the thorns of which go into the temples. Streams of Blood flow from His august head which mingle on His face with the hideous spitting from the filthy soldiery. Reduced to this state, the new Isaac must Himself carry the wood on which He is to be immolated, this heavy cross on which He is going to die. All that remains of His strength He uses to raise up and to drag the cruel and ignominious burden. But each effort reopens and dilates His Wounds; His Blood flows in abundance; exhausted He succumbs and three times He falls to the ground. Who can say how painful these falls are? It is then that Mary can finally approach her Divine Son. Ah! She would like to share the burden of the cross with her Jesus. But she is cruelly rejected by the soldiers. Her presence, instead

---

23   i.e. 'this reality' – he seems to say here it is rare when the workings of our imagination making up or exaggerating foreseen evils actually come to pass as bad as we imagined them.

of being a relief for her Son, was only an added sorrow.

And I refuse to carry my part of this cross which Jesus carried solely for me, which I alone deserved and which I alone should carry entirely. If I loved Jesus and Mary, I would at least resign myself to the little annoyances that each day presents to me, and which are only a part of the true cross.

The Religious Saints and Mary

St. Francis Xavier, to satisfy his piety towards Mary, braved the fury of the demons. More than once at night he was beaten by these hellish spirits while he was praying before an image of the Blessed Virgin. He propagated the devotion of the Immaculate Conception, along with the Christian faith. He vowed to maintain until death that Mary was conceived without sin.

Bl. Peter Canisius, apostle of Germany and the 'hammer of heresy', conceived the happy idea of rallying young people under the banner of Mary in those pious associations known since then under the name of the Congregation of the Blessed Virgin. The city of Fribourg in Switzerland, which was the scene of the last works of the apostolic man, is proud to still have a congregation established by Bl. Canisius himself.

Bl. Alphonse Rodriquez from his earliest childhood devoted his dearest delights to honouring Mary. It was by her help that he overcame the most violent temptations. Often the Mother of God favoured him with her presence and her conversations. He always defended the privilege of the Immaculate

Conception of the Blessed Virgin. He was seen constantly engaged in reciting the rosary, and his fingers bore the mark of his assiduity in this holy exercise. He peacefully expired while pronouncing the holy names of Jesus and Mary.

ഇ⊛ଓ

21. The Fifth Sorrow – The Cross

Contemplate Mary standing near the cross. Her heart is both enveloped and penetrated by an immense sorrow. *Abyssus abyssum invocat.* ("Deep calleth on deep", Psalm 41:8)** The abyss of suffering into which the Son is plunged calls for another abyss, the abyss of compassion where in her turn it is as though the mother is swallowed up.

Wanting to announce and figure in advance the sacrifice that Mary was to make on Calvary, God did not dare, it seems, to choose a woman. Anne, it is true, offers her son Samuel; but Samuel will be a priest and not a victim. A mother witnesses the horrendous ordeal of her seven sons, supporting them with her firm words as much as with her presence.[24] But it is for

---

**   Psalm 41 expresses affliction in tribulation, and is of course prophetic of the Passion. The word for 'deep' can also be literally translated as 'abyss', which Fr. de Boylesve then refers to.

24   A reference to the mother in the second book of Machabees who witnessed the horrific martyrdom of her seven sons before she was martyred in her turn. She courageously encouraged them to die well and not break God's law.

them eternal salvation. When it comes to a sacrifice requested for the salvation of others, to test the devotion, the generosity, the obedience of which human nature can be capable, God chooses not a woman, but a man, not a mother, but a father, and a man already tried by long patience, a man endowed with a hope against all hope; he is called Abraham, He orders him to sacrifice Isaac, his darling son, his only son. Then, as if He feared to break this man so strong by the consummation of the sacrifice, he stops the arm which is already rising to strike and He accepts the will as a *fait accompli.*

"Ah!" a woman once cried upon hearing about the order Abraham received to immolate his own son himself – surely God would never have given such a command to a mother! However, God did. Mary, I know, was not ordered to strike her Divine Son herself; but she would witness standing, in the attitude of the priest, an immolation of which that of Isaac would have been but a shadow.

First of all, who could compare Isaac to Jesus? Who could compare the tenderness of Abraham for Isaac to that of Mary for Jesus? Then, a single blow would have completed the sacrifice of the son of Abraham; but the sacrifice of Jesus is a torture which sums up all the pains and all the kinds of suffering of which man is susceptible.

Do you want to appreciate what the presence of Jesus on the cross was with regards to the pain and suffering of Mary? Remember that, according to St. William of Paris, "Mary loved Jesus so much that there is no pure creature who can love Him more," because, according to St. Amadeus, "Mary loved Jesus with a supernatural love as her God, and with a supernatural love as her Son." So Richard of St. Lawrence assures us that "the Seraphim could come down from heaven, to learn from the heart of Mary to love God." But all their ardour combined does not equal a single spark of that double and indivisible love by which Mary loves in Jesus, both her God and her Son. St. Bernadine points out that on Calvary "the fire of love with which this maternal heart burned turned into a sea of pain." And St. Bonaventure gives the reason, saying that "all the wounds strewn on the body of Jesus were concentrated in the heart of Mary."

It is therefore at Calvary, above all, that the reality surpasses all that the imagination and fear could have glimpsed in the prediction of Simeon the elder. If only Mary's eyes could detach themselves from this heartbreaking spectacle for a moment; but a mother's eye cannot close on the pains of her son. She knows that her presence, she knows that her gaze redoubles the suffering of Jesus; but how could she not be there? How could she look away from her crucified Jesus, or cease to suffer with Him for a moment?

However, stirred up by the enemies of Jesus, a frenzied multitude feeds on the spectacle of the sufferings and ignominy of Him who has done only good. And Mary hears the blasphemies, the cruel mockeries, the ironic challenges addressed to her Divine Son who answers the insults only with silence.

Jesus, however, speaks from the height of the cross. His first word is forgiveness for His tormentors. Mary, in her heart, joins in this forgiveness.

Another word of Jesus is addressed to Mary herself, 'Woman, behold thy son.' Surely Jesus could not choose for Mary a son more worthy to replace Him than the beloved disciple. However, what an exchange! In place of Jesus, what a son! Besides, here St. John is not alone; he represents all men and therefore all sinners, that is to say precisely, the murderers of Jesus. Mary finds in her maternal heart the strength to adopt them for her sons and to see in them the brothers of her Jesus. It is through them, it is true, that Jesus is crucified, but it is also for them, or rather, by the love which makes Him endure everything to save them is He crucified. - In the meantime, Mary will lose her only Son and in a few moments she will have no more sons, she will have no other sons than the executioners of her only Son.

"I thirst," and Mary can provide no relief from the burning thirst that is devouring the august Victim. This external and sensible thirst was a figure for another still more cruel, the thirst for the salvation of so many souls who will persist in refusing grace and who will make the torture of the cross useless for them. – Mary shares with her Son this ardent thirst, this desire for the salvation of obstinate sinners who are now her children and the brothers of her Jesus.

"My God, my God, why has Thou forsaken Me?" At this cry of desolation, no doubt Mary responds from the bottom of her heart with a new protest never to abandon this beloved Son that God Himself seems to have delivered to the executioners.

"All is consummated." A double sentiment then shares the heart of Mary. All is consummated; a little longer, Jesus will cease to suffer, and this thought should relieve the immense passion of the mother; but the suffering of Jesus will cease only with His death, and if the last breath of the Son is the end of His sorrowful Passion, it will also be the separation between the Son and the Mother. And at that moment Mary will have no other son but the sinner, who is the murderer of her only Son and of her Beloved.

"Father, into Thy hands I commend My spirit."

That said, Jesus utters a loud cry, His Heart breaks and is broken under the strain of all the pains that overwhelm His body and soul. – He is dead. – The sword has done its duty; the heart of the Mother is pierced right through, and the spear which will soon pass through the Heart of Jesus already dead on the cross will be felt only by the heart of Mary.

What are our sorrows compared to this immense sorrow!

ഇ ❀ ‌ଓ

The Three Patrons of the Youth

St Aloysius Gonzaga was born under a special protection of the Blessed Virgin. Therefore, he loved her like his mother. At the name of Mary he burst into tears. At the age of nine, he made a vow of virginity in her honour. At fifteen, he received from Mary herself the order to enter into the Company of Jesus (the Jesuits), where he lived like an angel.

St. Stanislaus Kostka loved the Blessed Virgin as a son loves his mother. Having fallen ill, Mary appeared to him and placed the Divine Child in his arms. It was then that he was ordered to enter the Company of Jesus. He wrote to his Heavenly Mother to obtain the grace to die on the day of the Assumption and it was granted him.

Bl. Jean Berchmans liked to recall that his birth had taken place on a Saturday.[+] From early on he made a vow of virginity to devote himself to the Queen

+ The day dedicated to Our Lady.

of Virgins. Having been admitted to the Congregation of Mary, he left no stone unturned to win her many loyal servants. On the verge of dying, he took in his hands the crucifix, the rosary and the book of Rules of the Company of Jesus, saying; "With these three objects, I gladly die."

ℰᏧ❀ᏽ

22. The Sixth Sorrow –
The Descent from the Cross

Nicodemus and Joseph of Arimathea took the bloodied Body of Jesus down from the cross. Mary received It on her knees. As with a child she pressed It to her heart with so much solicitude, respect and tenderness! Ah! In what a state they have put It! Approach, and with Mary consider this, and if you can, count the wounds with which this Body is covered ... Approach ... Ah! Rather, you do not approach. You are careful not to show yourself. Judas, Caiaphas, Pilate, the populace, the executioners, are not the only murderers of the Son of Mary. The murderer is the sinner; would you dare lay your hand on this Body and swear that you are innocent of this murder?

Let us come closer though and show ourselves to Mary. On earth she has no other son left but us. Of these two sons (us and Jesus), it is true, one killed the other, but far from desiring the death of the fratricide, Mary asks God the Father for grace for the new Cain while still covered with the Blood of the true Abel. This

Blood does not cry for vengeance, It cries for mercy. Seeing us clothed with the Blood of her Jesus, with this Blood which we shed but which was shed for us, she loves us out of love for her Son as He loved us Himself; she loves us as the dying Jesus wanted her to love us when He said to her, showing us to her in the person of St. John: "Woman behold thy son." Also like Jesus, she is ready to die for us; and if necessary, she would be ready to sacrifice this beloved Son again for us.

Let us therefore approach with shame, but with confidence; with sorrow, but with love; with fear, but with hope. Let us approach Mary, even when she holds in her arms this Son whom we have just sacrificed; but let us not forget our Mother's moans. If we are not allowed to swear that we are innocent of the death of Him who made Himself our brother, at least let us swear that we will not renew His death by our sins.

The Saint-Kings and Mary

St. Henry, Emperor, upon barely entering a town, liked to visit a church dedicated to Mary. Often he spent the whole night in front of her altars. One night being in Rome while he was keeping vigil in the church of Saint Mary-Major, he received from the Blessed Virgin the kiss of peace, through the ministry of an angel. We know that in agreement with St. Cunégonde his spouse, he kept perpetual virginity.

St. Stephen, King and Apostle of Hungary, was completely devoted to Mary. His mother had been told in advance by the Blessed Virgin of the birth of this blessed son. Stephen erected two bishoprics, he built several temples in honour of the Mother of God, and finally offered all his kingdom to the Queen of Heaven, begging her to regard it as her treasure and her inheritance.

St. Edward, King of England, seeing his kingdom ravaged by the Danes, put it under the protection of Mary. He could not fail to be heard, he who had promised never to refuse what would be asked of him in the name of the most Blessed Virgin, he who like Mary, kept virginity in marriage. (*Surius*).

St. Edmund, King of England, prayed continually before an image of Mary that he loved dearly. He was taken into a church and put to death in hatred of the faith. His head was hidden in a forest, but there came forth a cry that cause it to be discovered. It was returned to the body to which it reattached itself. (*Mayr*). [25]

ℬ ✣ ℭ

---

25   The St. Edmund was killed by Viking raiders who attempted to make him renounce his Faith in vain and shot him with arrows before decapitating him. They then threw his head into a briar patch in the woods. According to the tradition surrounding his death, it is said the king's followers later tried to find his head in vain until they heard a cry yelling out, 'Here! Here! Here!' in Latin. They discovered a wolf was guarding it, and assumed the wolf had miraculously called out the cry alerting them to its location. (EA. Bucc.)

23. The Seventh Sorrow – The Sepulchre

For the Son, the sepulchre is a sweet rest. This rest is obscure, it is true, but soon from the darkness of the tomb will spring the glory of the Resurrection, which is to erase forever the opprobrium of the cross. *Et erit sepulcrum ejus gloriosum.* ("And his sepulchre shall be glorious." - Isaiah 11:10) Already, the soul of Jesus begins to manifest His power in the midst of hell.[26]

For Mary it is not so. The agony of Calvary ceased only to give way to unspeakable desolation. The Body of Jesus is transported; Mary follows It. To see this sacred Body, to contemplate the wounds which cover It, such is the only consolation which remains to her. But when this Holy Body has been buried and placed in the tomb, especially when the stone which closes the entrance to the cave has been rolled in place, then Mary finds herself alone in this world. To be separated from her Son, for her it was death. Meditate often on this desolation, on this solitude of Mary.

---

26 I.e. Hell also encompasses the lower regions of the earth, and not just the hell of the damned. Christ descended to the Hell of the just souls in Limbo to release them, an event that has also been called the 'Harrowing of Hell'.

You are alone; men have abandoned or betrayed you. Your friends do not dare to declare themselves for you; they blush at you or they fear to compromise themselves by taking up your defence. Your enemies triumph. God Himself seems to have withdrawn from you. All is lost. There is no more hope. Discouragement and sadness have invaded your soul. –

Remember Mary.

For her, too, there was a time when all was lost. Unite your solitude with her solitude, your abandonment with her abandonment, your desolation with her desolation. But do not forget that between 'all is lost' and 'all is saved', there are only three days.

The Saint-Kings and Mary (Continued)

St. Ferdinand, King of Castile, always had an Image of Mary in his camp, and he attributed all his victories to the Queen of Heaven, relying more on her help over that of his most powerful allies. He desired to be buried at the foot of an image of the Most Blessed Virgin.

St. Ladislaus, King of Poland,[**] when marching in combat had in his hand a sword and a rosary. He was always victorious. After his death, his body transported itself without help from anyone to a church he had built in honour of Mary.

St. Louis, King of France, owed his birth to the prayers that Blanche, his mother, had addressed to Mary. He never forgot it. Every day he recited the Office of the Blessed Virgin. Every Saturday he washed and kissed the feet of three poor people. He built three churches in her honour. Mary appeared to him during a storm and said to him: "Fear not, I will be your help."

ℰ ❀ ℬ

[**] He was born in Poland, but elected King of Hungary and Croatia. (EA. Bucc.)

24. The Passion

I hail thee, generous Princess; I hail thee, thou, Rose of martyrs; I hail thee, Lilly of virgins! With whom canst thou be compared, O daughter of Jerusalem? How can thou be consoled, daughter of Zion? Thy sorrow is as immense as the ocean.

Around me, enemies have multiplied: (Psalm 24:19) people are rising up against me on all sides; my life is consumed in sorrow, my years are spent in moans; my heart melts within me like wax, (Psalm 21:15) and my tears are my daily bread; (Psalm 41:4) my soul is troubled, and Thou Lord, how long wilt Thou forsake me?

Come, O my soul, let us climb the mountain of the Lord. In front of this cross, in front of this tomb, a Mother weeps for her Son, and what Son? In desolation, she does not let a word escape from her: but those slowly flowing tears and this very silence tell us: 'See if there be any sorrow like unto my sorrow': *Videts si est dolor sicut dolor meus.* (Lamentations 1:12)

O Jesus, during Thy Passion the prediction of Simeon was fulfilled, and the sword of sorrow pierced the so sweet of soul of the glorious Virgin our Mother. Do, I beg of Thee, that after having remembered with respectful devotion the sorrows of her whom I received as a mother, that it be granted to me to receive the blessed fruits of Thy Passion.

Let us finally understand this: if it was necessary for Christ to suffer to enter into His glory,[+] if it was

---

+   "Then he said to them: O foolish, and slow of heart to

necessary for Mary to share the sufferings of her Son to share His glory, we cannot hope for an exception. Under a Head crowned with thorns, a member (of that Body) has no right to live in delights; the son of a Mother of Sorrow, born from the very sorrow of his Mother, cannot live in the joys of this world.[27] This language seems harsh: *Durus est hic sermo*; ("This saying is hard", John 6:61) but it ensures happiness. Happiness, in fact, consists more in giving than in receiving: *Beatius est magis dare quam accipere.* ("It is a more blessed thing to give, rather than to receive." Acts 20:35) Now, sacrifice is the gift *par excellence*; but sacrifice presupposes suffering, and suffering is the test by which generosity, disinterestedness, constancy are recognized. So accept suffering not only with resignation, but with joy. And remember that the more you give, the more you will be given: *Date et dabitur vobis.* (Luke 6:38) Give yourself to God, sacrifice yourself for God. God cannot allow Himself to be outdone: He will give Himself to you, completely and forever.

No, God cannot be outdone in generosity. Mary's fidelity to correspond to the singular graces of which she had been forewarned[**] obliges the Divine

---

believe in all things which the prophets have spoken. Ought not Christ to have suffered these things, and so to enter into his glory? And beginning at Moses and all the prophets, he expounded to them in all the scriptures, the things that were concerning him." (Luke 24:25-27)

27   I.e. we were made her children through the sorrow of the Passion wrought for our salvation, we cannot expect to be a child born of that great sorrow and expect salvation without sorrow and suffering. The Cross is the only path back to Heaven.

**   I.e. of the suffering she would undergo as Mother of the Saviour as she understood from the prophecies the cruel

Magnificence to crown her gifts with even more sublime gifts. These new gifts can be summed up in these three great privileges; 1st - Universal Motherhood; 2nd – her glorious Assumption; 3rd - Supreme Royalty.

The Saints and Mary

St. Mary Mary Magdalene became attached first to Our Lord, then to His Blessed Mother; she followed her everywhere, on her travels, to the foot of the cross, and in solitude after the death of Jesus. She raised a church in honour of Jesus Christ and another in honour of His Mother. (*Salmeron.*)

St. Cecilia, by her angelic virginity, merited a singular protection from the Mother of God. In an apparition she declared that the Lombards would not find her body thanks to the intervention of her august Sovereign, the Ever Virgin Mother of God. (*Nadasi.*)

St. Catherine (of Alexandria), virgin and martyr, was not yet a Christian when Mary deigned to appear and presented her Divine Son. But the Infant Jesus did not want to be given to Catherine because she was not baptised. After her baptism the saint received once again a visit from Mary and her Son. Jesus gave her a ring as a pledge of the covenant He made with her soul. This Divine Spouse gave her the strength to confound in a dispute nearly fifty pagans.

ജ❀ന

suffering the Redeemer would endure.

25. Her Universal Motherhood

The moment when the sacrifice reaches its extreme limit is usually the moment when the glory which is to crown it commences. It is at the time Abraham raises his arm to sacrifice Isaac that God stops him and promises that from Isaac will come the blessing of the world; it is at the moment when believing Joseph has lost his life, Jacob sees all his sorrows renewed which is brought to a climax by the departure of his Benjamin, it is then that Joseph is restored to him in all the splendour of his glory; it is at the moment when Joseph regards himself as forgotten forever that he is called to the first rank of the court of Pharaoh; it is at the moment when Job's sufferings reach the highest degree that God justifies him, heals him, gives him back double all that he had lost; it is at the moment when Moses sinks more than ever into the solitude and silence of the desert that God calls him and gives him the mission which will make him the greatest personage of the Old Testament; it is at the moment when Tobias, overwhelmed under the weight of the test and asks only for death that an angel from heaven is sent to restore him happiness and peace.

Mary is standing by the cross. In a dying voice, Jesus completes His own sacrifice and at the same time He consummates that of His Mother. "Woman," He told her, "behold thy son." He no longer calls her His Mother. *Woman!* This word is the supreme blow which was to separate two Hearts, two Souls, which made one Heart and one Soul - "Behold thy son". It must be that, in the person of John, Mary must adopt for her son the murderers of her Jesus. But in this same word, upon completing the sacrifice, the compensation begins. Mary sacrificed her only and beloved Son, she had the courage to adopt the murderers of that cherished Son; immediately by the effective and all powerful virtue of the Word which raised the world from nothingness, Mary becomes the Mother of all the elect. Now, in the supernatural order, in the order of grace, in the order of glory, she is the Mother of all those who will be saved by the Blood of her First Born, of all the beloved disciples of her Jesus.

Mary is therefore really our Mother, as Jesus is really our Brother. Such is indeed the title which He gives to His apostles, when after the resurrection He orders Magdalene to announce to them His next appearance; "Tell My brothers" - And so this title answers the truth. By baptism we put on Jesus Christ. Invested with Him, and thereby become similar to Him, we are like Him, not by nature it is true, but by grace and by adoption we are in name and in fact the sons of God: *Ut filii Dei nominemur and simus.* ("That we should be called, and should be the sons of God." - 1 John 3:1)

Through Holy Communion, intimately united with Jesus, we can say with St. Paul: "And I live, now not I; it is Jesus that lives in me." (Galatians 2:20)

Mary therefore sees in each of us her Jesus Whom we invested through baptism, Who abides and Who lives in us through Holy Communion; from then on she adopts us and loves us as she loves this beloved Son.

This is how Jesus' words are realised: "Woman, behold thy son." An efficacious word, I repeat, since it was spoken by the One for Whom to will is to do: *Quaecumque voluit fecit*; ("He hath done ... whatsoever

122

He would." Psalm 113:11) for Whom it suffices only to speak and the thing is done: *Dixit et facta sunt.* ("He spoke and they were made." Psalms 32:9) Universal Motherhood, such is the first glory by which God rewards Mary's fidelity to the graces of which He had forewarned her.

The Saints and Mary (Continued)

St. Ursula, virgin and martyr, knew how to inspire love towards the Mother of God in her companions. At the time of their martyrdom the angels were seen presenting their souls to God and to the Most Blessed Virgin. Mary herself deigned to dictate to Bl. Herman the story of the massacre of these heroic virgins.

St. Genevieve, virgin, had the custom to spend Saturday nights in prayer to the Mother of God. One evening the wind extinguished the torch that lit the way to the Church of the Most Blessed Virgin. But it lit up again as soon as she had even touched it. A child who she helped to recite the praises of Mary having died, Genevieve resurrected him.

St. Clotilde obtained the conversion of Clovis (the first King of France) by the prayers she never ceased to address to the Blessed Virgin. It was in effect Mary who brought the life of the Faith to the Eldest Daughter of the Church. We can attribute the example of Clotilde for the zeal that France has never ceased to display for the cult of devotion to the Queen of Heaven.

St. Radegone, spouse of King Clotaire, then a religious, fasted for forty days every year in honour of the Mother of God. Every Saturday she washed the heads of lepers with her hands when she encountered any, and she gave food to beggars. She had the name of Mary engraved on her body. (*Fastes de Marie*)

ഇ ❀ ങ

26. Her Death

To respond to her Divine Son's wishes and to fulfil her duties as Universal Mother of the elect, Mary resigned herself to remaining on earth after the Ascension of Jesus. As during an earlier time when she watched over the cradle of the Infant-God, so she will watch over the cradle of the nascent Church. She will help the apostles and the first faithful with her advice and especially with her examples.

However, her heart is in heaven, her mind is on her Jesus. This Divine Sun attracts her unceasingly and detaches her more and more from this earth.

I seem to hear the sweet voice of Jesus calling His Mother: "Come, the crown awaits you," *Veni, coronaberis*; (Canticles 4:8) and Mary, responding: "Come, Jesus, my Son and my Lord," *Veni, Domine, Jesus* (Apoc. 22:20); and Jesus resuming in His turn: "Yes, I come, and I come quickly:" *Etiam venio cito.* (Apoc. 22:20) Mary is therefore going to die.

Miraculously transported to the dying Virgin, the Apostles surround her. Already they have received from her the last blessings. Mary has fulfilled her

mission. Her soul is detached from her body without pain, without illness, without agony. The Queen of Martyrs won her crown at the foot of the cross.

Now she dies from the desire to contemplate the glory of this beloved Son Whom she once saw expire in shame and torment. For so long her thoughts, her affections have been in heaven! After the death of her Son, after the glorious Ascension of this beloved Son, the Mother called for death; for her death will not be a separation, it will be the Mother's reunion with the Son.

Why do we fear death? This is because we only live for the earth and for the times. What folly to go through such trouble for what we will have to leave behind tomorrow!

Death would be sweet for us, if with St. Paul we could say: "I die daily", *quotidie morior.* (1 Cor. 15:31) Let us die every day to our earthly and sensual affections; every day detach ourselves from the earth, from men, from our body; let us become more and more attached to heaven every day; to Jesus: then instead of being for us an object of terror, death will be the end of our desires. For it will be the passage from earth to heaven, from time to eternity; the moment which will separate our soul from our body will be the one which will reunite it forever to Jesus, and our last breath will be like the last and supreme outpouring of our heart to God.

The Saints and Mary (Continued)

St. Bridget[28] was only seven years old when she received a crown from the Mother of God. Later, Mary favoured her with a great number of revelations. One day the Blessed Virgin speaking in regard to her clients[29] said to her: "I see their sorrows and their labours; I will visit them at death and I will place them with me in the heavenly abode." The saint inspired the love of Mary in her children to the point that Charles, her son, said: "I would rather suffer the torments of hell than to see taken away from Mary the glory of her Divine Maternity," and that blessed Catherine, her daughter, would recite the 'Hail Mary' before each of her actions, and also before responding to people who consulted her. - At the time of his death, Charles was defended against demons by Mary, who then let Bridget know that this beloved son enjoyed heavenly happiness. - Catherine was favoured by a vision in which the world appeared to her as enveloped in flames which were going to consume it if Mary had not interceded.

St. Mechtilde, virgin, once saw Our Lord Jesus Christ recommending her to His Blessed Mother. Mary let her know that no prayer was more pleasing to her than the Angelic Salutation, (the Hail Mary). She promised to assist her at death, if every day she recited three Hail Marys in honour of the omnipotent power of the Father, the wisdom of the Son and the infinite love of the Holy Spirit. (See the Appendix regarding this

---

28 St. Bridget of Sweden.
29 i.e. of those devoted to her.

devotion.)

St. Clare made a vow of virginity in the Church of the Portiuncula. By the steadfastness of her footsteps towards Mary she deserved her sweetest favours. The Holy Mother, escorted by a choir of virgins, assisted her at the moment of her death, and having kissed her tenderly, she covered her with a rich mantle and led her to the Divine Bridegroom.

ഇ⊕ଓ

27. The Funeral Solemnities

The holy women prepared the funeral ceremony. Escorted by the apostles and by the faithful, the body of Mary is placed in the tomb. The angels combine their concerts with the songs of the Christians. For three days the celestial harmonies were heard; on the third day the hymn ceased. It was only then that the apostle St. Thomas was present with his colleagues. God had allowed this delay to manifest the glory of Mary. Sorrowful for not having attended the last moments of the Mother of Jesus, Thomas requested the favour to venerate at least the mortal remains of the Blessed Virgin. At his urging, the tomb is opened. But, oh what a surprise! The body of Mary is no longer there: *Non est hic.*

Holy apostles, why do you seek among the dead the one who gave life to the very Author of Life?

Conceived without sin, preserved from the contagion of original sin, she was not subject to the law of death, and if to imitate her Son she could like Him die of love, like Him she had to be preserved from the corruption of the tomb, like Him she was to be resurrected without waiting for the day of the General Resurrection.

Mother of the Word Incarnate, in return for the temporal life she gave Him, she was to receive immortal life from Him.

Between the Mother and the Son the resemblance had always been perfect, it had to be up to the end, and like Jesus, Mary was to be resurrected on the third day after her happy death.

Purified from sin and delivered from eternal death by baptism, we are not to fear temporal death. For us, as for Mary, this death is but a passage from time into eternity. Having become the living members of Jesus by Holy Communion, we receive from there a life which assures us of a glorious resurrection. Let us be faithful, one day it will be granted to us to join our Mother.

The Saints and Mary (Continued)

St. Catherine of Sienna made a vow of virginity at the age of seven. Heaven showed her a fiery lily that did not burn. One day she was severely reprimanded by the Mother of God for a very slight fault. Another time she was busy baking bread, Mary appeared to her and helped her with her work. When she went up the stairs she recited an *Ave Maria* at each step.

St. Teresa (of Avila) after losing her mother, chose the Mother of Jesus to replace hers. One day

Mary hung a precious jewel around her neck, urging her to continue to honour St. Joseph with special devotion. It was under the patronage of Mary and Joseph that Teresa undertook the reform of Carmel, (i.e. of the Carmelite order).

St. Madeleine de Pazzi had a special devotion to the mystery of the Annunciation; St. Augustine engraved on her heart in letters of gold these words of St. John: "And the Word was made flesh." One day when she was besieged with bad thoughts, she had recourse to the Blessed Virgin. Mary clothed her with a white veil and delivered her from the stings of the flesh. God the Father further promised her that the Blessed Mother would protect her.

෨ ✾ ര

28. The Assumption

We continue with the thought of Mary's triumph, when resurrected by the virtue of her Divine Son, escorted by angels, she made her solemn entry into Heaven.

On her arrival the angels who surround the throne of His Thrice Holy Majesty, all cry out together: "What is this admirable creature who advances like the dawn, beautiful as the moon, brilliant as the sun, terrible as an army in battle array?" (Canticles 6:9)

And the angels escorting Mary answer: "Open the eternal doors, rise up, and let in the Queen of glory."**

"Who is this Queen of glory?" reprise the Princes of Heaven.

"It is the Mother of the Lord," reply the angels surrounding August Mary; "it is the Mother of He Who is Power itself, of He Who has triumphed by the Cross. Open your ranks, let the Queen of virtues, the Queen of glory pass."

The heavens were opened. The patriarchs advance and they hardly dare to greet their daughter in this Virgin so brilliant who after having crushed the head of the serpent, gave to the world He in whom all the nations were to be blessed.

The prophets can no longer find words to exalt a glory whose brilliance effaces all the splendours of their prophetic images of her. Mary has passed through the ranks of the patriarchs and the prophets, she arrives at the angelic choirs.

"Rise up," the angels of the last choir cry, "go up higher: God has entrusted us with the care of men; but to thee He entrusted the care of God made Man."

"Rise up," the Archangels exclaim: "God has charged us to lead the superiors of human associations; but thou led the first steps of the King of all kings."

"Rise up," cry the Principalities; "God has committed to us the custody of human communities; but thou, O celestial Princess, thou will be the Queen of the entire Church."

** Fr. De Boylesve aptly imagines the Queen of Heaven greeted the same way as her Son in Psalm 23: "Lift up your gates, O ye princes, and be ye lifted up, O eternal gates: and the King of Glory shall enter in."

"Rise, rise again," the angelic Powers cry: "Our mission is to preside over the government of the celestial suns and to fight the infernal powers; while all the powers of hell, of the earth and of Heaven tremblingly obey the one who commanded the Sun of Truth, the Sun of Justice."

"Rise, rise again," cry the angelic Virtues; "It is through us that God works miracles; but a word from thy mouth determined the first miracle of Him Whom we are only ministers."

"Rise up," repeat in their turn the angelical Dominations; "Through us God directs the heavenly militias; but thou art the sovereign, the ruler as thy name declares, and thou hast commanded the Ruler of rulers."

"Rise up," resume the Thrones; "Upon us rests the majesty of the Thrice Holy God; but thou wert the living throne of the King of kings Whom thou didst carry on thy breast and in thine arms."

"Rise up," the Cherubim cry; "Through us God illuminates all intelligences; but it is through thee henceforth that we will receive the lights of the Word, it is in thy heart that we will find the words of Wisdom Incarnate that thou didst collect and preserve with so much care."

"Rise up," the Seraphims cry: "Through us God embraces all wills with the ardour of charity; from now on, we will go draw the flames of Divine Love from thy heart in order to spread them in all souls."

Then the seven angels who constantly stand before the Divine Majesty withdraw to open a passage for the Mother of their King. Would it not be permissible to suppose that, in the Name of the Trinity of Which he was once the ambassador, that the

Archangel Gabriel greeted Mary by once again addressing her with the words of his first greeting: "Hail Mary, full of grace, the Lord is with thee, blessed art thou among women?"

Then also undoubtedly the leader of the celestial militias, the Archangel Michael, came to present to his sovereign the homage of the angelic armies and to declare that henceforth it would be from her, the Mother of Jesus, that he would ask for the orders of the King of kings.

To all these greetings Mary replied with the words of her admirable canticle: *Magnificat anima mea Dominum.* (My soul doth magnify the Lord.)

At last, she is at the foot of the throne of the August Trinity. Jesus then presents His Mother to His Heavenly Father; and the Father recognizes in Mary His beloved daughter; and the Son recognizes in Mary His beloved Mother, and the Holy Spirit recognizes in Mary His beloved spouse; and the Father, the Son and the Holy Spirit crown Mary Queen of Heaven and earth, of men and of angels.

Seated at the right hand of her Son, she shines above every pure creature, above the stars of the firmament, above the patriarchs and prophets, above the apostles, the martyrs, the doctors, the virgins, above the Angels, the Dominations and the Seraphim. What are all earthly human pomps when compared with the immortal radiance of celestial glories?

Happy is he who has lived in darkness and contempt on earth!

Do you want to be exalted for eternity, humble yourself in these times, erase yourself, disappear.

Live in Heaven. There is your Mother. On earth there is no real joy for you. Far from his mother, a child cannot be happy. The memory of the death of

Mary and of her glorious Assumption will therefore complete your detachment from the pleasures and vanities of this present life.

Mary, Mother of Jesus and our Mother, I beseech thee, by thy sweet death, to obtain for me an easy and happy death. At this decisive moment come in person to assist thy child, come and receive this soul with its last breath. By thy glorious Assumption, obtain for me a grace which frees me from the goods and evils of the earth and of the times, and which lifts me above the fears and vain hopes of this world. Obtain for me the grace to enter immediately after my death into the participation of thy joy. Oh! When will it be granted to me to contemplate thy glory and that of thy Divine Son!

ಬಿ ✿ ಬಿ

Our Lady of La Salette - The Apparition

On the 19th of September 1846, two poor children of the little burg of Corps in the diocese of Grenoble had been sent as usual to the mountain of La Salette to graze cows. One was called Maximin and was eleven years old; the other child was a small girl of fourteen years named Mélanie. It was a Saturday and the day before the feast of Our Lady of the Seven Sorrows.

The children asleep next to the stream

Provided with their small provisions the two children met up, leading their herds. The weather was magnificent. Around noon, to the distant sound of the Angelus, they sat down to take their poor meal near a spring which at that time was dry. Then they fell asleep some distance from each other.

Mélanie was the first to wake up. No longer seeing her cows, she called Maximin and they both went away, leaving their little sacks near the spring. Having found their herds not far away, they come back to collect their bags. Suddenly Melanie sees from afar, on the side of the spring, a light brighter than the sun, but not of the same colour. "Come see," she shouts to Maximin; "Come quickly see a light over there!"

"Where is it?" replied little Maximin, hurrying up. Mélanie pointed to the spring.

Then, say the children, the light opened, and in the middle they saw a Lady sitting on a stone with her feet in the dry bed of that spring. Her attitude announced great pain: there she was, her head in her hands, her elbows resting on her knees. She spreads her hands: her face seemed bathed in tears; but those tears were brilliant; they did not fall to the ground: they disappeared like sparks of fire.

The figure of the mysterious Lady was so radiant with light that the children were dazzled by it. Maximin could not stare at her; Mélanie looked at her, but it was with great difficulty. Her forehead was surrounded by a crown of roses and a brilliant diadem of stars above which rose a sort of mitre slightly curved forward. A white thin cloth, also adorned with garlands of roses, covered her chest. Her dress, studded with stars and pearls, was dazzlingly white; and in front it was covered with a sort of apron which looked like gold. Her shoes were also white, adorned with glittering roses. From the midst of the roses which covered this mysterious ornament, a kind of flame sprang up, which rose like incense, and mingled with the radiant light with which the Lady was surrounded.

A great brilliant chain, three fingers wide, ran down the wreath of roses; and from a smaller chain hung a golden crucifix: the cross shone brightly; to the right and to the left, they saw pincers and a hammer which seemed to be hanging on to nothing. The brilliance of Christ was even more splendid than that of the cross.

଼୦❀ର

29. Her Universal Royalty

The royalty of Mary is not just a simple title of honour. After her Assumption, her royal action has not ceased to be exercised over all the Church. I am not speaking only of converted sinners and of the righteous preserved by her all-powerful intercession; the Church itself recognizes that it owes all the triumphs it has won over the enemies of Jesus to her special assistance. *Cunctas haereses sola ineremisti in universo mundo.* It is thou, O Mary, who alone have exterminated all the heresies of the entire world. - Travel through the Catholic countries: at every step you will encounter shrines, altars, statues, there under one title, here under another, they attest to the royal intervention of Mary.

But in becoming our Queen, Mary does not cease to be our Mother, and if she rejoices in her elevation and greatness, it is mainly because her power gives her the means to help those children who are all the more dear to her the more unhappy they are.

Let us therefore rejoice in the glory of our Mother, for her and for us. Let us add our felicitations to those she receives from the saints, the angels, from God Himself, and let us not tire of thanking the Divine Majesty for her exaltation.

Thou art great, O Mary! Thou art the Mother of Jesus, but thou art good, thou art always my Mother. I adore God only, I adore Jesus only: but I venerate thee, O Mary, and after God, thou art the most worthy object of my homage. How could I not honour her whom

Jesus honours as His Mother, and whom the Heavenly Father has raised above all creation? I hope from God alone the graces I need, but I only expect them through Mary. I do not want anything that has not passed through my Mother's hands. It is through her that I will ask for everything I desire; for she is all-powerful by the very power of God, for she is all good by the very goodness of God.

<u>Our Lady of La Salette – The Warning</u>

Meanwhile the Lady rises, folds her arms, and in a caressing voice soft as heavenly music: "Fear not, my children," she said to them. "Come; I am here to bring you important news." Reassured, the two little shepherds approach; from her side the Blessed Virgin advances towards them. In a few steps, they found themselves in front of her, one beside the other.

The Mother of Mercy, still shedding tears, then said to them: "If my people will not submit I shall be compelled to let go the arm of my Son. It is so heavy and so powerful that I can no longer sustain it. For how long have I suffered on your behalf! You will never be able to to acknowledge the pains that I have taken over you."[30]

---

30   Some translations differ regarding the message of the apparition. For instance, this sentence is usually translated as: "Pray as much as you like, do as much as you like, but you will never be able to repay me for the trouble I have taken over you." Also there appears to be some parts of Our Lady's message left out of this account by Fr. De Boylesve for the sake of brevity. See the Appendix for the full message.

"I gave you six days to work; I reserved the seventh for Myself, and no one wants to grant it to Me! This is what weighs down my Son's arm so much. Those who drive the carts only swear and blaspheme the Name of my Son. These are the two things that weigh heavily on the arm of my Son! If the harvest fails, you are the cause." Then the Blessed Virgin announced various plagues that would be all the punishment for the sins of men, and in particular for blasphemies and the violation of the Sunday rest. She then gave each of the children a secret: and although she spoke aloud, Mélanie did not hear what she was saying to Maximin, nor Maximin what she was saying to Mélanie; they only saw the movement of her lips

These two secrets, written later and sealed by the Order of the Bishop of Grenoble, were brought to the Pope, (Bl. Pius IX), who read them and appeared to be greatly moved. One of them concerned Paris and France; the other, if I remember correctly, was relating to Rome and to Pius IX himself. They announced punishments and misfortunes if the world did not convert. [31]

The Blessed Virgin added: "Are you saying your prayers well, my children?" - "No, Madame, *pas quére*," Maximin responded frankly. - "Ah! My children, they must be done well, evening and morning; when you don't have time, just say one Our Father and an Hail Mary, and when you have the time, say more."

The Blessed Virgin went on to speak of the contempt that so many people have of the Mass, and especially of the Sunday Mass, of the brazen violation

---

31   See the Appendix for the newly discovered original version of the secrets that were sent to the pope in 1851.

of the Church laws regarding abstinence and the Lenten fast. And she ended by saying in a grave voice, "My children, you will pass this on to my people." She repeated this order twice. - Shortly after she disappeared.

A beautiful church has since been erected where the Blessed Virgin left the two children to rise to heaven and disappear. Graces without number, dazzling and sudden healings have made it one of the most famous pilgrimages in the Catholic world. The dried up spring, which previously flowed only at intervals, still flows now; and the water which gushes from it operates every day, one can say it without exaggeration, obvious miraculous effects. In the country, an admirable change immediately took place, mainly in the way of the sanctification of Sunday, the respect of the holy Name of GOD, and the observance of the commandments of the Church. (Taken from the *Month of Mary by Mgr. De Ségur.*)

℘ ❀ ℀

30. The Secret of Her Grandeur

Who will tell us how, without doing anything extraordinary in the eyes of men, Mary achieved the highest degree of glory that a simple creature can attain? Who will reveal to us the secret of her greatness? Jesus will tell us.

One day when the crowd gathered around Him, He was told that His Mother and brothers wanted to speak to Him. "And who is my mother, who are my brothers," Jesus replied? "The one who listens to My

words and who puts them into practice, the one who does what My Heavenly Father wants, this one is My mother, My brother, My sister." (Mark 3:35, Matt. 12:50)

Now, Mary has gathered the words of Jesus, and even His smallest actions, considering them in her heart: *Maria autem conservabat omnia verba haec conferens in cordon suo.* ("But Mary kept all these words, pondering them in her heart." Luke 2:19) Mary declared herself the servant, saying to the envoy of God: "Be it done to me according to thy word." *Fiat mihi secundum verbum tuum.* There is the secret of her greatness and her glory.

Seek in all the good pleasure and glory of God, and you will participate in the honour of the Divine Maternity. But do not focus on yourself. Have great ideas, conceive big plans, but forget yourself, spend yourselves for the glory of God and for the salvation of souls. The desire for the glory of God will bring you, like Mary Magdalene, back to the feet of Jesus; the desire for the salvation of souls will inspire you to the activity of Martha: it is the union of these two lives that makes the perfection and the greatness of Mary, Mother of Jesus and our Mother.

Mother of Jesus, she remains near her Son, she watches over the cradle of the Divine Child, she follows Him in all His steps, she stands near His cross.

Mother of men, to support the nascent Church, she consented to stay on this earth and to spend many years here, far from Heaven where her Jesus reigns in glory.

May our entire life be spent between work, prayer and suffering! Heaven will be the prize.

O my Mother! O my Queen! Mother, thou art full of kindness for thy children; Queen, thou art all-powerful to defend them and to rescue them. I put all my trust in thee, certain that I will not be confounded. *In te, Domina, speravi, non confundar in aeternum.* (Psalm 30:2)

ℬ ✤ ℭ

Our Lady of Lourdes

First Apparition of Mary to Bernadette – February 11, 1858

Her vesture was graceful and simple: a white robe; a long white veil descending from her head with large folds; a blue belt fluttering below the knees; on each of her bare feet a bright, blooming yellow rose. The child struck down with surprise and affirmation, uncertain, rubs her eyes, looks again ... The Lady smiled delightfully at her from the midst of the light. Falling on her knees, Bernadette grabs her rosary, carries the cross to her forehead to sign herself, but her hand comes down as if paralysed. So, the Apparition, taking the golden crucifix from a rosary that she wore, made a large sign of the cross on herself. The child can then sign. The Lady folds her hands and runs the white beads of her long rosary between her fingers, the yellow chain of which sparkles; her lips did not move. The child imitates this attitude and these movements, and recites the *Ave Marias* with her rosary. The mysterious Lady invites her with a gesture to approach, but she does not dare. Finally, the ever smiling Vision disappears.

The Chapel, the Spring

One day the Lady gave an order to Bernadette: "Go tell the priests that a chapel must be built here and that they must come here in procession." The child takes this word to the parish priest of Lourdes; later she received the same command again. In the middle of the fortnight, the Vision, showing the end of the grotto, said; "Go drink from the spring and wash yourself there; you will eat of the grass that is there." Bernadette obeyed. But at the place indicated there was no spring, she barely saw any humidity. On a sign from the Lady, she makes a small hole in the dirt, and a little muddy water collects at the bottom. With the palm of her hand, she brings it to her lips three times without daring to touch it. Finally, after another glance towards the niche, she drinks this disgusting mixture, then she wets her face with it and goes to eat a few leaves of a grass which was growing nearby.

At the same time the Lady said to Bernadette again: "You will pray for the conversion of sinners ... You will kiss the earth for the conversion of sinners."

And the child was seen to ascend on her knees the slope which rose below the niche, repeating: "Penance! Penance!" She was seen to place her lips on the ground.

After that, she had to climb the incline of the cave several times in atonement for sinners and often kiss the earth; she was again ordered to go and drink, but the water had increased, she filled her hand with it more and more times and drank it in without difficulty.

Apparition of March 25, 1858.

Bernadette returned to the grotto on the 25th of March, the Feast of the Annunciation, and found a huge crowd there. The Lady appeared to her in the same brilliant glory and with the same benignity. Towards the end of the ecstasy, the child asked for her name two times; two long smiles alone answered her. She insisted. At this third prayer, the Lady smiled again, then separates her crossed hands at the height of the belt, raises them, joins them in front of her breast in a gesture of divine majesty and grace, and with eyes towards the sky she says, "I am the Immaculate Conception." - After which she disappeared.

The child kept this memory of another world, but did not understand the phrase 'Immaculate Conception', which she heard for the first time.

The Last Apparition, July 16

The crowds continued to flow to the grotto and prayed unceasingly; but the civil authority, claiming to prevent a *superstition* from rooting, after having taken the advice of the minister of public worship, closed the entrance to the rock with a plank fence and prohibited access on pain of a fine. The people braved this defence. There were reports of judicial convictions.

St. Bernadette

The 16th of July, the Feast of Our Lady of Mt. Carmel, Bernadette, going to pray in front of the rock on the opposite bank of the Gave, had seen again more splendid than ever, and for the last time, the vision of the celestial Lady.

The Canonical Judgement

The increasingly famous grotto attracted ever-resurgent waves of pilgrims. Often, here and there, they saw a new miracle shine forth. Finally, after long studies, in which theology and science examined everything, the apparitions, the cures attributed to the water of the grotto, the Bishop of Tarbes pronounced his judgement. On the 18th of January 1862, he proclaimed that the Lady that appeared to Bernadette was really IMMACULATE MARY, MOTHER OF GOD, and authorized public devotion to Our Lady of Lourdes. (*Extract from the Notice of Approval by Mgr. De Tarbes.*)

ജ ❀ ര

31. Homage and Consecration

O Mary conceived without sin, Immaculate Virgin, Mother of Jesus and Our Mother, Queen of Heaven and earth!

We thank God for the three main graces for which, by a singular privilege, thou wert pre-sanctified:

From all Eternity thou wert predestined to be the Mother of the Word Incarnate;

By an anticipated application of the merits of thy Divine Son, thou wert preserved from Original sin;

Thou wert born miraculously and full of grace.

We praise thee for thy fidelity in corresponding to the graces for which God had pre-sanctified thee:

First, by thy consecration, that, at three years of age that thou didst make of thyself and of thy whole entire life, on the day of thy Presentation;

Then, by thy faith and by the humble obedience to the word of the Archangel Gabriel on the day of the Annunciation,

Finally, by the sacrifice that thou didst made of thy Jesus when presenting Him to His Father on the day of thy Purification, a sacrifice that thou didst fully consummate at the foot of the Cross.

We praise God for the glory with which He rewarded thy fidelity to the graces for which He had pre-sanctified thee.

For the glory of God and for the salvation of the world, thou didst sacrifice thy only and beloved Son, this Divine Son thou didst give for thy children, of all the elect, then He surrendered Himself to thee, full of life and glory.

Thou didst keep without stain thy original purity; thou didst consent to receive in thy chaste womb God made Man, thou didst not know the corruption of the tomb, but like thy Divine Son, three days after thy death, thou wert resurrected to be brought up to Heaven.

When the angel came to offer thee along with the honour of Divine Maternity the immense sorrows attached to this high dignity, thou replied that thou wert nothing but the handmaid of the Lord; on the day of thy Assumption, the Eternal Father crowned thee His Immaculate Daughter, the Word Incarnate crowned thee His Beloved Mother, the Holy Spirit crowned thee His virginal Spouse: the entire Trinity unites to crown thee Queen of earth and Heaven, Sovereign of men and of the angels.

O Virgin, our Mother and our Queen! We consecrate to thee this day our bodies and souls, our minds and our hearts, our thoughts and our desires, our words and our works, our labour and our sufferings, our life and our death, our parents, our relations, our friends, our earthly country and our spiritual country, France[32] and the Church. We beseech thee to admit us under thy standard, under the cross and thy Divine Son, and that we may obtain from His Sacred Heart the light and strength to answer His call with generous dedication to the holy Church our Mother, the salvation of souls, and the glory of the most Holy Trinity. So be it. Amen.

---

32   Fr. De Boylesve was French, and France is where this book was originally published, therefore France is named. You may name your country here.

Mary and the Revolution

Pius VII, in the depths of the prison where revolutionary impiety had retained him captive, addressed his prayers to Mary: the oppressor toppled, the Pope is freed.

Pius IX, chased from Rome, he also by Revolution, implored in his turn the succour of the Immaculate Virgin, and the sword of France brings him back to the Eternal City. The grateful Pontiff proclaims the dogma of the Immaculate Conception: the entire Church applauds, and shortly after Mary shows herself at Lourdes, and when asked to give her name, she replies: "I am the Immaculate Conception."

REGNUM GALLIAE – REGNUN MARIAE
NUNQUAM PERIBIT.

(The Kingdom of Gaul (France) – Kingdom of Mary,
Shall never perish.)

ꕥ ❀ ꕥ

HYMNS

ꕥ ❀ ꕥꕥ ❀ ꕥꕥ ❀ ꕥ

<u>Mary and the Church</u>

Let's set off, leave the port behind;
Let us hoist the sail,
In the dark night we see the star shine,
I recognize Mary, hail!
Let us brave our end.

<u>Chorus:</u> Lord, when it comes to Thy glory,
We will sail against the waves:
 Mary ensures the victory:
 Onward sailors, courage!

More terrible than the sea
Its furies the world prepares.
We are the children, the soldiers of Mary,
We will defy the storms infernal.

Chorus: Lord, etc.

Villains, your sinister looks
 In vain announce the thunder;
On you this day the children declare war.
Through them the Virgin lays low your banners.

Chorus: Lord, etc.

The villains promised me liberty!
Yes, I am free and desire to be.
Jesus alone is my King, my Master alone is He;
Get back, children of the century and of impiety!

Chorus: Lord, etc.

How I despise your contempt!
Your false promises make me smile.
Ah! Little do I esteem what the world admires;
And for that price my heart is too high to sell.

Chorus: Lord, etc.

(English approximation of the original French text by Fr. Marin de Boylesve, music was composed by P. Lambillotte and was originally sold at Graff, 84, Rue Bonaparte, Paris. E.A. Bucc.)

ഔ ✿ ౫

France to Mary

To thy feet, Immaculate Virgin
Thou seest thy children run,
By thy smile so consoling,
France never will perish.

Refrain:

Yes, forever in France, Mary
Alone with Jesus will reign;
No, no, never shall our homeland,
Lucifer obey.

Black hell spreads its sail
Over the dark ocean waves,
But to the Franks thou wilt be the star
During the night of the hurricane.
Refrain: Yes .... etc.

Breaking the yoke of Babylon,
France recognizes thy law;
Offering thee the sceptre and crown,
To thee France pledges her faith.
Refrain: Yes ... etc.

Arranged around thy banner
We will know how to defend thy rights;
For thy Son and for His Vicar,
See, France takes back the Cross.
Refrain: Yes ... etc.

But thou who gives the victory
Over the world and over Hell,
For the Pope who defended thy glory
When wilt thou break the chains?
Refrain: Yes ... etc.

By prostrate repentance,
The heart knows with just fear,
To perish France is condemned,
May it recognize its King, thy Son!
Refrain: Yes ... etc.

Under the flag of victory
Our warriors to thee will return;
Walking in the shade of thy glory,
Their laurels they will offer.
Refrain: Yes ... etc.

At the canons stationed,
Under thy banner's folds,
The Church shall France defend
By a single flash of its gaze.
Refrain: Yes ... etc.

To the Mother, the Eldest Daughter
Shall bring aid in your name;
And finally when crowned in glory,
Will keep her rank forever.
Refrain: Yes ... etc.

(English approximation of the original French text by Fr. Marin de Boylesve, music was composed by Fr. A. de A. and printed / sold at Paris, Haton, 33, Rue Bonaparte. E.A. Bucc.)

ഔ ✿ ൠ

Our Lady of La Salette

What did you see on the mountain,
Little shepherds, can you tell us?
What did you see in the countryside?
Speak, children, of what are you afraid?
We have heard from Mary;
We have seen flow her tears:
God our homeland threatens
With misfortunes most frightful!

Duo: To the Virgin of La Salette,
Swear, swear upon your honour
the feast days to respect,
And the blessed Name of the Lord.

Chorus: Our Lady of La Salette
Upon our honour we swear to thee
the feast days to respect
And the blessed Name of the Lord.

Do you hear the thunderbolt rumble
Of a God justly abraded?
He prepares to reduce to dust
The workers of iniquity.
A day of prayer God commands:
But these times said: No rest!
For the poor there are no wages
If for one day he ceases his work.

Duo: To the Virgin, etc

What is this reckless voice
That, with a blasphemy so daring,
Defies the God of thunder,
Cursing the Name of Heaven's King?
To this cry the holy phalanges say:
Death to the blasphemer!
But suddenly the Queen of Angels
Throws herself at the feet of God the Saviour.

Duo: To the Virgin, etc.

'Leave them,' Jesus says to His Mother:
'Men believe themselves to be gods;
Their hearts incline to the earth,
Barefaced the heavens they threaten:
In silence the rest of them follow.
Gold has become the new Baal;
They no longer teach their children
But only that cult of a cold metal. '

Duo: To the Virgin, etc.

'My Son,' resumes the Mother august,
'My Son, forgive them again;
If before that ephemeral idol
The numerous slaves of gold
In their indifference so mindless
Have so cowardly bowed their heads,
I see more than seven thousand
In France who never shall bend.'

Duo: To the Virgin, etc.

(English approximation of the original French text by
Fr. Marin de Boylesve, music by P. Lambillotte. - Chants à
Marie, Poussielgue. E.A. Bucc.)

ഇ ✿ ℃ഇ ✿ ℃ഇ ✿ ℃

St. Thomas Becket

APPENDIX

ഇ❀ര഻ഇ❀ര഻ഇ❀ര഻

<u>Devotion of the Seven Temporal and Seven Celestial Joys of Our Lady</u>

While there are various forms of honouring the Joys of Our Lady in the Middle Ages, since Fr. de Boylesve mentions the devotion of St. Thomas Becket of Canterbury in particular, we shall relate his story here.

St Thomas was devoted to saying seven Hail Marys in honour of her Temporal Joys on earth. These Seven Temporal Joys have usually been listed as:

1. The Annunciation
2. The Nativity of Jesus
3. The Adoration of the Magi,
4. The Resurrection of Christ,
5. The Ascension of Christ,
6. Pentecost: Descent of the Holy Spirit (or the Assumption according to the version attributed to St. Thomas.)
7. The Coronation of Our Lady

However, Our Lady appeared to St. Thomas and directed her Celestial Joys should also be honoured, saying:

"Why are you glad only for my joys which were temporal, and do not rather rejoice over the present joys which I now enjoy in heaven, which are eternal?

Rejoice, therefore, and exult with me for the future.

First, because my glory surpasses the happiness of all the Saints.

Secondly, because as the sun gives light to the day, so my brightness gives light to the whole court of heaven.

Thirdly, because all the hosts of heaven obey me, and ever honour me.

Fourthly, because my Son and I have but one will.

Fifthly, because God rewards, at my pleasure, all my servants, both now and hereafter.

Sixthly, because I sit next to the Holy Trinity, and my body is glorified.

Seventhly, because I am certainly sure that these joys will last forever, and never end.

And whoever shall honour me by rejoicing in these my joys, shall receive the consolation of my presence at the departure of his soul from the body, and I will free his soul from evil enemies, and I will present him in the sight of my Son, that he may possess with me the everlasting joys of Paradise."

She then asked him to say seven extra Hail Marys in honour of her Celestial Joys in addition to those of the Temporal Joys.

According to tradition, St. Thomas composed the following hymn in honour of the Seven Temporal and Seven Heavenly Joys of Our Lady, or, they have been attributed to him. Apparently, to gain the graces, it is necessary to say an Ave Maria (Hail Mary) with each verse for both the Temporal and Heavenly Joys.

The Latin is included below first, then the English translation.

The Temporal or Earthly Joys

Gaude, Virgo, Mater Christi,
Quem per aurem (auram?) concepisti,
Gabriele nuntio: (*Ave Maria*)

Gaude, quia Deo plena
Peperisti sine poena,
Cum pudoris lilio: (*Ave Maria*)

Gaude, quia Magi dona
Tuo Nato ferunt bona,
Quem tenes in gremio: (*Ave Maria*)

Guade, quia tui Nati
Quem dolebas morte pati
Fulget resurrectio: (*Ave Maria*)

Gaude, Christo ascendente
Et in coelum te tuente
Cum Sanctorum nubilo: (*Ave Maria*)

Gaude, quae post Christum scandis,
Et est tibi honor grandis
In coeli palatio. (*Ave Maria*)

Ubi fructus ventris tui,
Nobis detur per te frui,
In perenni gaudio.
Alleluia. (*Ave Maria*)

The Seven Celestial Joys

Gaude flore virginali
Quae honore speciali
Transcendis splendiferum
Angelorum principatum,
Et sanctorum decoratum
Dignitate munerum. (*Ave Maria*)

Gaude Sponsa cara Dei,
Nam ut lux clara diei
Solis datur lumine,
Sic tu facis orbem vere
Tuae pacis resplendere
Lucis plenitudine. (*Ave Maria*)

Gaude, splendens vas virtutum,
Tuae sedis est ad nutum
Tota coeli curia:
Te benignam et felicem
Jesu dignam Genitricem
Veneratur gloria. (*Ave Maria*)

Gaude, nexu voluntatis
Et amplexu charitatis
Juncta sic altissimo
Ut ad nutum consequaris
Quicquid, Virgo, postularis
A Jesus dilectissimo. (*Ave Maria*)

Gaude, mater miserorum,
Quia Pater praemiorum
Dabit te colentibus
Congruentem hic mercedem,
Et felicem poli sedem
Sursum in coelestibus. (*Ave Maria*)

Gaude, humilis beata,
Corpore glorificata,
Meruisti maxima
Flore tantae dignitatis
Ut sis Sanctae Trinitatis
Sessione proxima. (*Ave Maria*)

Gaude Virgo, Mater pura,
Certa manens et secura
Quod heac tua gaudia
Non cessabunt, non durescent,
Sed durabunt et florescent
In perenni gloria. Amen. (Ave Maria)

V. Exaltata es Sancta Dei Genitrix,
R. Super choros Angelorum ad coelestia regna.

<u>Oremus:</u>

O dulcissime Jesu Christe, qui beatissimam Geniticem Tuam, gloriosam Virginem Mariam perpetuis gaudiis in coelo laetificasti, concede propitius ut ejus meritis et precibus continuis, salutem et prosperitatem mentis et corporis consequaperveniamus aeternam. Per Te, Jesus Christe, Salvator mundi, qui vivis et regnas cum Deo Patre in unitate Spiritus Sancti Deus per omnia saecula saeculorum. Amen. [33]

❁

Translation

The Temporal or Earthly Joys

1. The Annunciation

Rejoice, virgin Mother of Christ
who hast conceived by ear,
with Gabriel as messenger. (*Hail Mary*).

---

[33] 'The Life and Martyrdom of Saint Thomas Becket, Archbishop of Canterbury and Legate of the Holy See', John Morris, (Longman, Brown, Green, Longmans, Roberts, London, 1859), pp. 383-384.

2. The Nativity

Rejoice, for full of God
thou gavest birth without pain,
with the lily of purity. (*Hail Mary*)

3. The Adoration of the Magi

Rejoice, for the gifts of the wise men
Good things they bring thy Son
Whom thou dost hold in thy lap. (*Hail Mary*)

4. The Resurrection

Rejoice, for the resurrection
of thy Son now shines,
Whose death thou mourned, (*Hail Mary*)

5. The Ascension

Rejoice, as Christ ascends,
and, in thy sight, is carried
into heaven by His own strength. (*Hail Mary*)

6. The Assumption

Rejoice, thou who riseth after Him
and to whom great honour is due
in the palace of heaven, (*Hail Mary*)

7. The Coronation

Where the fruit of thy womb
is granted us, through thee, to enjoy
in eternal rejoicing.
Alleluia.   (*Hail Mary*)

The Celestial Joys

1. Her Glory Surpassing the Angels and Saints

Rejoice in the virginal flower,
and special honour,
surpassing the magnificent
leader of the angels
and the host of saints
adorned with worthiness. (*Hail Mary*)

2. The Brightness of Her Glory

Rejoice, dear spouse of God,
for as the bright light of day
is given by the lamp of the sun,
so thou truly make the circle
of thy peace shine
in the fullness of light. (*Hail Mary*)

3. Her Authority as Queen in Heaven

Rejoice, splendid vessel of virtue,
for whose nod waits
the whole court of heaven.
Thou, kind and blessed,
Worthy mother of Jesus
Are venerated in glory. (*Hail Mary*)

4. Her Complete Union of Will with Jesus

Rejoice in the binding of will
and the embrace of love
thus joined in the highest,
that thou art faithful to thy vow
whatever, O virgin, is asked of thee
by sweetest Jesus. (*Hail Mary*)

5. The Lord's Generosity to Her Servants

Rejoice, Mother of Mercy,
for the Father of the Ages
will give those who honour thee
appropriate reward here in the world
and a blessed throne
to be rulers in the heavens. (*Hail Mary*)

6. Her Exalted Place Next to the Trinity

Rejoice, humble blessed one,
Thy body glorified,
Thy merit the greatest,
Flower of such dignity
That thou may be to the Holy Trinity
seated nearest.

7. The Everlasting Perpetuity
of Her Celestial Joys

Rejoice, pure virgin Mother,
Remaining certain and secure,
That these seven joys
Will neither end nor decrease
But will last and flourish
Through eternal ages. (*Hail Mary*)

V. The holy Mother of God has gone up
to the heavenly kingdom,

R. Above the choirs of angels:

<u>Let us pray</u>:

Oh sweetest Jesus Christ, Thou Who hast blessed Thy Mother, the glorious Virgin Mary, in heaven by perpetual joys, mercifully grant that by her continued merits and prayers we may obtain eternal health and well-being of mind and body. Through Thee, Jesus Christ, Saviour of the world, who liveth and reignth with God the Father in the unity of the Holy Spirit, God forever and ever. Amen.

The Brown Scapular of
Our Lady of Mount Carmel

A Brief History of the Carmelites

In the Old Testament, the ancient prophets had devout followers who joined communities or 'schools', called 'Schools of the Prophets', which were a prefigurement of what would be religious communities today.

In the early centuries, a Christian community in the spirit of Elias the prophet founded an order on Mt. Carmel, the mountain where Elias battled with the pagan priests of Baal and where heavenly fire came and consumed his sacrifice. It is also where he had a vision of Our Lady, the promised Woman who would crush the head of the serpent. In the same spirit of Elias the habit of the early Christian order was brown like the camel hair he wore, and, the order was dedicated to Our Lady. They lived a meditative life there for centuries, until the Muslim Saracens began their bloody persecutions. Many were martyred, others fled to various regions such as Sicily, France and England, as well as other parts of Europe.

However, they still felt the sting of persecution and misunderstanding from the ecclesiastical authorities in the countries they fled to. The newcomers were perceived as a 'new order' and therefore looked upon with suspicion when in fact the order was not new, while those who knew differently believed the spirituality of the meditative order was not compatible in other Christian countries once they had left their territory of Carmel, that basically, there was no room or need for such an order outside Mt. Carmel.

St. Simon Stock
and the Revelation of the Scapular

St. Simon was born in Kent, England c. 1165. From an early age he felt the call to become a hermit and so when he was twelve he left home and lived an austere life in the woods, his home a hollowed out tree trunk, his food the wild herbs he could find. He was one of the first aspirants to enter the Carmelite order upon its arrival at Kent, no doubt the contemplative and austere life of the order attracted him. His reputation for sanctity spread in the order, and he was elected the first Prior-General of the Carmelites in the West in 1245.

However, as General of the Order of the "Brothers of the Blessed Virgin Mary", he was grieved by the bitter opposition against them, from the heartbreaking persecutions launched by the Saracens in the East, to the bitter prejudices they faced in the West. He defended the order against the unjust attacks, praying to Our Lady and practising austere penances for help. Then during a night vigil on July 16, 1251 he ardently prayed: "Flower of Carmel, Blossoming Vine, Brightness of Heaven, Solitary Virgin Mother, though without knowledge of man yet a meek Mother, grant special favour to the Carmelites, O Star of the Sea."

His prayer was answered. Our Lady appeared

with a heavenly retinue, and holding the habit of their order, the scapular, she offered it to him and said: "Beloved son, receive this scapular of your Order, token of my confraternity, as a guarantee of the privilege which I have obtained for you and all Carmelites. Whosoever shall die wearing it shall not suffer eternal fire. It is a sign of salvation, a safeguard in perils, a covenant of peace, a token of my special protection until the end of time."

The Blessed Virgin then advised him to appeal to the Pope to obtain assistance in their troubles.

Therefore, the Brown Scapular is a special sign of Our Lady's protection, and that her intercession will save those who wear it from eternal fire, that is, obtain for that soul the grace of final perseverance, and protection from many spiritual and also temporal dangers.

The Addition of the Sabbatine Privilege.

According to the Bull of Pope John XXII, the Blessed Virgin appeared to him and gave an additional promise to those who wear the Brown Scapular, saying, "I, the Mother of Grace, shall descend on the Saturday after their death and whomsoever I shall find in purgatory I shall free so that I may lead them to the holy mountain of life everlasting."

However Our Lady gave certain requirements that must be followed to obtain the Sabbatine Privilege.

1.   Wear the Brown Scapular continuously. (One must be formally enrolled.)

2.   Observe chastity according to one's state in life (married /single).

3. Recite daily the Little Office of the Blessed Virgin, OR Observe the fasts of the Church together with abstaining from meat on Wednesdays and Saturdays, OR with the permission of a priest, say five decades of Our Lady's Most Holy Rosary OR, with the permission of a priest substitute some other good work.

Questions and Answers
about the Brown Scapular

What are the conditions for gaining the Our Lady's promise of the Brown Scapular?

1.) To observe exactly what has been prescribed regarding material, colour, and shape of the Scapular, that is it must be brown 100% woven sheep's wool in a rectangular shape. (Although black is also permitted.) The wool must be woven, it cannot be of a smashed felt with the fibres unwoven, (note: this sounds confusing, but felted wool is fine, which is woven wool fuzzed up and looks like felt, but it is woven). The scapular cannot be made of any other cloth. Other types of cloth are strictly forbidden. The straps, however, can be of cloth or even chains, but the main rectangular pieces of the cloth must be woven sheep wool. The shape must be rectangular or square, it cannot be oval, round, or polygonal. There can be a pious holy image on the scapular, such as Our Lady of Mt. Carmel or the Carmelite shield. However, the picture should not completely cover the brown, there should be a plentiful brown edge left so the scapular can be recognised for what it is. In other words, the brown (or black) wool must predominate the scapular.

2.) To be enrolled in the Scapular confraternity by a priest.

3.) To wear it continually.

Please note that there are no special prayers or good works that are necessary to receive the promise of salvation from eternal fire. The Scapular is a silent prayer that shows a person's complete consecration and dedication to the Blessed Virgin Mary. The Scapular is a devotion whereby we venerate Her, love Her, and trust in Her protection, and we tell Her these things every moment of the day by simply wearing the Brown Scapular.

However, for the Sabbatine privilege, see the requirements above.

Who may be invested in the Brown Scapular?

All the Catholic faithful should be enrolled. It is customary for children to be enrolled after their First Holy Communion, but even infants can be invested.

How do I enrol in the Brown Scapular?

Any priest can enrol or invest you in the Brown Scapular. There is a special formula of investiture that the priest performs. The formula is included in the next section after the Questions and Answers.

Who can enrol me in the Brown Scapular?

Any Catholic priest can enrol you. It was once customary that only the Carmelite Fathers were permitted to enrol the lay faithful, and special permission was needed for any other priest to perform the ceremony. However, this devotion has spread so far and wide throughout the Catholic world that now the Church has given permission to all priests to invest the faithful in the Brown Scapular.

What is the Confraternity of the Brown Scapular?

Once invested in the Scapular a person automatically becomes a member of the Confraternity of the Brown Scapular. What is meant by the Confraternity is that having been enrolled in the Scapular, you belong to a spiritual family whereby you have the privilege of being affiliated with the Carmelite Order, participating in the merits of the Carmelite Fathers and Religious in life and in death, as well as receiving the promises of Our Lady through the

Scapular. Although at one time it was customary to inscribe one's name in the Confraternity Register (the parish priest would do this for all those he enrolled by sending the names to a Carmelite convent where the Confraternity was canonically erected), it is no longer the practice to do so. Part of the reason for this is that the Scapular has become, thanks be to God, such a universal sacramental and devotion that the Church has taken away this obligation upon the lay faithful. It is sufficient to be invested in the Scapular to be a member of the Confraternity.

How do I enrol in the Confraternity?

By being invested in the Brown Scapular by a priest.

Can an ordained deacon enrol a person in the Brown Scapular?

No, an ordained deacon cannot enrol a person in the Scapular. Only an ordained priest of the Catholic Church can perform the investiture.

How must I wear the Scapular in order to receive its benefits?

You must wear it over the shoulders so that one part hangs over your chest and the other side hangs over the back. Both parts cannot be carried in the front or the back, otherwise, the wearer runs the risk of not receiving the promise.

May the Scapular be fastened or pinned to my clothing?

The Scapular must hang over the shoulders with one side hanging in the front and the other side hanging in the back. However, one may sew or pin the scapular to an undergarment to hold it in place or to keep it from rising about one's neck.

What if I'm allergic to wool?

If one has a serious allergy to wool or has irritation of the skin, one can wear the wool scapular over one's clothing, encase the wool scapular in plastic, or wear the Scapular Medal with an image of the Sacred Heart on one side and an image of Our Lady on the other side. (Please see the question about the Scapular Medal).

Does the Scapular have to be touching the skin?

No, it may be worn over or under any part of the clothing.

May one wear a different
colour of the Scapular?

Different colour Scapulars do exist as sacramentals in the Church for other devotions, such as the Red Scapular in honour of Our Lord's Passion. However, the Brown Scapular that the lay faithful wear is a miniature of the Carmelite Religious Habit, and since that Habit is brown in colour, it has always been regarded as the proper colour for the Scapular. However, black wool is permissible.

Must I always wear the Scapular
or may I take it off?

In order to receive the promise, the Scapular must always be worn. We must understand that by wearing the Scapular we show our consecration and devotion to the Blessed Virgin. Our Blessed Mother cannot be pleased in any one who out of vanity or fear takes it off whenever it is not convenient to wear it. By wearing it we make an open profession of our faith, confidence, and love of Her.

But, may I take my Scapular off to bathe?

Yes.

May I wear a Scapular Medal as a replacement for my Scapular?

No, the medal was not meant to be a regular replacement. However, St. Pius X and subsequent Popes, have declared that in <u>necessary cases such as in foreign or tropical climate missions</u>, the Scapular Medal with an image of the Sacred Heart on one side and an image of Our Lady on the other side may be worn instead of the wool Scapular,<u> this is usually due to the scarcity of sheep's wool in those countries, and is</u> *not meant to be the norm.*

The Scapular Medal can also be worn in case of *<u>real necessity or for very serious reasons,</u>* such as an allergy to wool. <u>But if the Scapular Medal is worn for insufficient reason, such as vanity or convenience, the wearer runs the risk of not receiving the benefit of the Scapular promise.</u> It is important to remember that the small Scapular worn by the lay faithful is meant to be a miniature version of what the Carmelites wear as part of their Religious Habit, which is never substituted for anything else.

If I need a new Scapular, do I need to be re-invested?

No. If your Scapular has worn out or has broken, you only need to get another one and start wearing it. The blessing and investiture is still valid for the new Scapular, since the blessing is predominately given to the *person* who is invested in the Scapular.

What are the indulgences granted to those who devoutly wear the Scapular?

1. A plenary indulgence on the day of receiving the Scapular. Conditions: Confession and Communion.

2. Plenary indulgence at the moment of death. Conditions: Confession, Communion, and devout invocation with the lips, or at least with the heart, of the Holy Name of Jesus.

3. Reciting the Office of the Blessed Virgin Mary devoutly – 100 days indulgence.

4. Each time the Scapular is kissed – 500 days indulgence.

THE INVESTITURE CEREMONY
(In Latin and English)

In Latin

Priest: Ostende nobis Domine misericordiam tuam.

Respondent: Et salutare tuum da nobis.

V. - Domine exaudi orationem meum.

R - Et clamor meus ad te veniat.

V. - Dominus vobiscum.

R - Et cum spiritu tuo.

V. - Oremus. Domine Jesu Christe, humani generis Salvator, hunc habitum, quem propter tuum tuaeque Genitricis Virginis Mariae de Monte Carmelo, Amorem servus tuus devote est delaturus, dextera tua sancti ✠ fica, tu eadem Genitrice tua intercedente, ab hoste maligno defensus in tua gratia usque ad mortem perseveret: Qui vivis et regnas in saecula saeculorum. Amen.

(The Priest blesses the scapular with holy water and the person(s) being enrolled. He then invests that person(s), saying:)

V. - Accipite hunc, habitum benedictum

precantes sanctissima Virginem, ut ejus meritis illum perferatis sine macula, et vos ab omni adversitate defendat, atque advitam perducat aeternam. Amen.

(After the investiture, the priest continues with the following prayers):

V. - Ego, ex potestate mihi concessa, recipio vos ad participationem, omnium bonorum spiritualium, qua, cooperante misericordia Jesu Christi, a Religiosa de Monte Carmelo peraguntur. In Nomine Patris ✠ et Filii ✠ et Spiritus Sancti. ✠ Amen.

Benedicat ✠ vos Conditor caeli at terrae, Deus omnipotens, qui vos cooptare dignatus est in Confraternitatem Beatae Mariae Virginis de Monte Carmelo: quam exoramus, ut in hore obitus vestri conterat caput serpentis antiqui, atque palmam et coronam sempiternae hereditatis tandem consequamini. Per Christum Dominum nostrum.

R - Amen.

(The priest again sprinkles the person(s) enrolled with holy water.)

(End of the Investiture ceremony.)

English

Priest: Show us, O Lord, Thy mercy.

Respondent: And grant us Thy salvation.

P - Lord, hear my prayer.

R - And let my cry come unto Thee.

P - The Lord be with you.

R - And with your Spirit.

P - Lord Jesus Christ, Saviour of the human race, sanctify ✠ by Thy power these scapulars, which for love of Thee and for love of Our Lady of Mount Carmel, Thy servants will wear devoutly, so that through the intercession of the same Virgin Mary, Mother of God, and protected against the evil spirit, they persevere until death in Thy grace. Thou who livest and reignest world without end. Amen.

(The Priest blesses the scapular with holy water and the person(s) being enrolled. He then invests that person(s), saying:)

P - Receive this blessed scapular and beseech the Blessed Virgin that through Her merits, you may wear it without stain. May it defend you against all adversity and accompany you to eternal life. Amen.

(After the investiture, the priest continues with the prayers:)

P - I, by the power vested in me, admit you to participate in all the spiritual benefits obtained through the mercy of Jesus Christ by the Religious Order of Mount Carmel. In the name of the Father ✠ and of the Son ✠ and of the Holy Ghost. ✠ Amen.

May God Almighty, the Creator of Heaven and earth, bless ✠ you, He who has deigned to join you to the Confraternity of the Blessed Virgin of Mount Carmel; we beseech Her to crush the head of the ancient serpent so that you may enter into possession of your eternal heritage through Christ our Lord.

R – Amen.

(Once more, the priest sprinkles the person(s) enrolled with holy water.)

ಐ❀ೕಐ❀ೕಐ❀ೕ

The Holy Rosary

(The following excerpts are from St. Marie-Louis de Montfort's famous spiritual classic, "The Secret of the Rosary".)

ॐ ✤ ॐ

What the Rosary Is

The Prayers of the Rosary

The Rosary is made up of two things: mental prayer and vocal prayer. In the Holy Rosary mental prayer is none other than meditation of the chief mysteries of the life, death and glory of Jesus Christ and of His Blessed Mother. Vocal prayer consists in saying fifteen decades of the Hail Mary, each decade headed by an Our Father, while at the same time meditating on and contemplating the fifteen principle virtues which Jesus and Mary practised in the fifteen mysteries of the Holy Rosary.

In the first five decades we must honour the five Joyous Mysteries and meditate on them, in the second five decades the Sorrowful Mysteries and in the third group of five, the Glorious Mysteries. So the Rosary is a blessed blending of mental and vocal prayer by which we honour and learn to imitate the mysteries and the virtues of the life, death, passion and glory of Jesus and Mary.

(Note: St. John Paul II in our times has recently added an additional set of mysteries to the Rosary between the Joyful and the Sorrowful: the Luminous Mysteries reflecting on the mysteries of Our Lord's ministry on earth. See the section 'How to Pray the Rosary' for more information. E.A. Bucc.)

Origin (of the Rosary)

Since the Holy Rosary is composed, principally and in substance, of the prayer of Christ and the Angelic Salutation, that is the Our Father and the Hail Mary, it was without doubt the first prayer and the first devotion of the faithful and has been in use all through the centuries, from the time of the apostles and disciples down to the present.

But it was only in the year 1214, however, that Holy Mother Church received the rosary in its present form and according to the method we use today. It was given to the Church by Saint Dominic who had received it from the Blessed Virgin as a powerful means of converting the Albigensians[34] and other sinners. (...)

---

34   The Albigensian heresy was also known as Catharism and had taken deep root in southern France in the middle ages. The Cathars believed that the physical tangible world was inherently corrupt and evil, therefore it was the *creation* of Satan, and that the 'good' realm was the spiritual one of God. They also believed that the universe was a battleground between good, which was spirit, and evil, which was matter. Since they believed all matter was evil and of Satan, they taught that human beings were good spirits trapped in 'evil' physical bodies and battling to be freed from this 'evil' body. However this contradicts the True Faith as Catholicism teaches God created everything, and all He created was good. Everything on earth was in a state of perfection, until Adam and Eve who were given free will chose evil of their own

Saint Dominic, seeing that the gravity of people's sins was hindering the conversion of the Albingensians, withdrew into a forest near Toulouse where he prayed unceasingly for three days and three nights. During this time he did nothing but weep and do harsh penances in order to appease the anger of Almighty God. He used his discipline so much that his body was lacerated, and finally he fell into a coma.

At this point Our Lady appeared to him, accompanied by three angels, and she said:

"Dear Dominic, do you know which weapon the Blessed Trinity wants to use to reform the world?"

"Oh, my Lady," answered Saint Dominic, "you know far better than I do because next to your Son Jesus Christ you have always been the chief instrument of our salvation."

Then Our Lady replied:

"I want you to know that, in this kind of warfare, the battering ram has always been the Angelic Psalter which is the foundation stone of the New Testament. Therefore if you want to reach these hardened souls and win them over to God, preach my Psalter."[35]

---

accord by falling to the Serpent's temptation, thereby bringing death and corruption into the world. While human nature is now fallen, the flesh is certainly not a creation of Satan, and, the bodies of the just will be glorified at the end of time and rejoined with soul. (E.A. Bucc.)

35   I.e. the original 'rosary' began with the hermits of the first centuries who were illiterate, who could not read nor had access to a copy of the book of Psalms, and therefore would recite an Our Father and Hail Mary for every psalm, and would keep count using stones, or stringing seeds on a cord. St. Dominic, after this famous vision of Our Lady, was the first who began the custom of saying 150 Hail Marys for the psalms, and it became known as the 'Psalter of Mary'. Later, when the devotion given to St. Dominic began to wane, it was re-established by Bl. Alan de la Roche in the 1460, the people

So he arose, comforted, and burning with zeal for the conversion of the people in that district he made straight for the Cathedral. At once unseen angels rang the bells to gather the people together and Saint Dominic began to preach.

At the very beginning of his sermon an appalling storm broke out, the earth shook, the sun was darkened, and there was so much thunder and lightning that all were very much afraid. Even greater was their fear when looking at a picture of Our Lady exposed in a prominent place they saw her raise her arms to heaven three times to call down God's vengeance upon them if they failed to be converted, to amend their lives, and seek the protection of the Holy Mother of God.

At last, at the prayer of Saint Dominic, the storm came to an end, and he went on preaching, So fervently and compellingly did he explain the importance and value of the Holy Rosary that almost all the people of Toulouse embraced it and renounced their false beliefs. In a very short time a great improvement was seen in the town; people began leading Christian lives and gave up their former bad habits. ("The Secret of the Rosary",Monfort Publications, Christ and Country Books, 1984, pp. 17-18)

---

than began to call it the 'Rosary' meaning 'Crown of Roses', an act of devotion of each Hail Mary crowning Our Lady with roses that would never fade. Our Lady approved of the new name, for various apparitions began to happen showing that indeed, each Hail Mary produced a rose, and each entire Rosary formed a crown for her. A Jesuit brother named Alphonsus Rodriguez used to say his rosary so devoutly and with such fervour he was shown that a red rose came out of his mouth at each Our Father, and a white one at each Hail Mary. See "The Secret of the Rosary".

The 15 Promises of the Rosary
Revealed by Our Lady
to St. Dominic and Bl. Alan de la Roche

- Those who faithfully serve me by the recitation of the Rosary shall receive signal graces.

- I promise my special protection and the greatest graces to all those who shall recite the Rosary.

- The Rosary shall be a powerful armour against hell. It will destroy vice, decrease sin, and defeat heresies.

- The recitation of the Rosary will cause virtue and good works to flourish. It will obtain for souls the abundant mercy of God. It will withdraw the hearts of men from the love of the world and its vanities, and will lift them to the desire of eternal things. Oh, that souls would sanctify themselves by this means.

- The soul which recommends itself to me by the recitation of the Rosary shall not perish.

- Those who recite my Rosary devoutly, applying themselves to the consideration of its sacred mysteries, shall never be conquered by misfortune. In his justice, God will not chastise them; nor shall they perish by an unprovided death. Sinners shall convert. The just shall persevere in grace and become worthy of eternal life.

- Those who have a true devotion to the Rosary shall not die without the sacraments of the Church.

- Those who faithfully recite the Rosary shall have, during their life and at their death, the light of God and the plenitude of His graces. At the moment of death, they shall participate in the merits of the saints in paradise.

- I shall deliver from purgatory those who have been devoted to the Rosary.

- The faithful children of the Rosary shall merit a high degree of glory in heaven.

- By the recitation of the Rosary you shall obtain all that you ask of me.

- Those who propagate the holy Rosary shall be aided by me in their necessities.

- I have obtained from my Divine Son that all the advocates of the Rosary shall have for intercessors the entire celestial court during their life and at the hour of their death.

- All who recite the Rosary are my beloved children and the brothers and sisters of my only Son, Jesus Christ.

- Devotion for my Rosary is a great sign of predestination.

The Benefits of the Rosary According to Bl. Alan de la Roche

*(Source: 'The Secret of the Rosary,'
by St. Louis de Monfort)*

- Sinners are forgiven.

- Souls that thirst are refreshed.

- Those who are fettered have their bonds broken.

- Those who weep find happiness.

- Those who are tempted find peace.

- The poor find help.

- Religious are reformed.

- Those who are ignorant are instructed.

- The living learn to overcome pride.

- The dead (the Holy souls) have their pains eased by suffrages.

The Results of the Rosary According to St. Louis de Montfort

"The Rosary recited with meditation on the mysteries brings about the following marvellous results:

1. It gradually gives us a perfect knowledge of Jesus Christ.
2. It purifies our souls, washing away sin;
3. It gives us victory over all our enemies;
4. It makes it easy for us to practise virtue;
5. It sets us on fire with love of Our Blessed Lord;
6. It enriches us with grace and merits.
7. It supplies us with what is needed to pay all our debts to God and to our fellow men, and finally, it obtains all kinds of graces for us from Almighty God.

The knowledge of Jesus Christ is the science of Christians and the science of salvation; St. Paul says that it surpasses all human sciences in value and perfection. (Cf. Philipp. 3:8) This is true:

1.) because of the dignity of its object, which is a God-man compared to Whom the whole universe is but a drop of dew or a grain of sand;
2.) because of its helpfulness to us; human sciences, on the other hand, but fill us with the smoke and emptiness of pride;
3.) and finally, because in its utter necessity; for no one can possibly be saved without knowledge of Jesus

Christ – and yet a man who knows absolutely nothing of any of the other sciences will be saved as long as he is illuminated by the sciences of Jesus Christ.

Blessed is the Rosary which gives us this science and knowledge of our Blessed Lord through our meditations on His life, death, passion and glory."

(*Note*: *St. Marie Louis de Monfort also relates the Rosary is a powerful protection against demons. The demons are so terrified of it that even the blessed beads of the sacramental itself terrifies them and sends them fleeing. People who suffered strong temptations found great relief from the demonic attacks simply by wearing a rosary around their neck, and, exorcists were able to drive demons away by placing a set of beads around the necks of the possessed. Our Lady also told Bl. Alan de la Roche she would grant even more graces to the members of the Archconfraternity of the Rosary if they wore their beads around their neck. See 'The Secret of the Rosary' by St. Louis de Monfort. Note, sacramentals such as a set of rosary beads must be blessed by a priest. E.A. Bucc.*)

The Archconfraternity of the Rosary[**]

In order to receive additional graces when

** Source: "Rosary Center and Confraternity"
https://rosarycenter.org/confraternity-obligations-benefits-and-promises

praying the rosary, it is strongly recommended that the faithful enrol in the Archconfraternity of the Rosary (or simply called the Confraternity) to avail of its benefits and additional indulgences. Before enrolling, please reach the obligations and benefits of the Confraternity. There is also a Rosary Confraternity prayer that must be said daily with the rosary.

The Obligations

- Each member must make an effort to pray the Fifteen Mysteries of the Rosary each week[1.] This means praying one Rosary each of the Joyful, Sorrowful, and Glorious mysteries (3 Rosaries) in the course of a **week.** If you already pray the rosary at least this often you do not need to add any additional rosaries during the week to fulfil this requirement. This requirement does not bind under sin, meaning, that if an enrolled member does not fulfil the obligation, it is **NOT** a sin, not even a venial one. Of course a member then misses out on the graces and blessings that would have come through their prayers.

- They must have his / her name inscribed in the register of the Confraternity.

There are no meetings, and no dues. As the members pray, they pray also for the intentions of all the other members of the Rosary Confraternity worldwide, living and deceased.

Since Pope St. John Paul II added the five

Luminous Mysteries, the members of the Confraternity are encouraged to include that extra weekly Rosary. However, at the time of this publication, there is as yet no official statement regarding this matter. Those who recite only the fifteen traditional mysteries will continue to share in the benefits of the Rosary Confraternity until some official source declares the contrary.

The Benefits of Being a Member

They receive:

1.) The special protection of the Mother of God.

2.) A share in the prayer of many hundreds of thousands of members the world over, even after death.

3.) A share in the prayers, Masses and apostolic works of the entire Order of Preachers. (i.e. the Dominicans).

4.) The intercession of the entire heavenly court.

5.) Various plenary and partial indulgences.

6.) Six times a year the Rosary Center publication "The Rosary, Light and Life" is sent to those members who wish it. Its purpose is to provide sound doctrine and spiritual guidance for readers everywhere.

The Indulgences

For members of the Rosary Confraternity, a plenary indulgence, under the usual conditions, is granted:

1.) On the day of enrolment. (When application is made, a certificate of membership is sent, depending where you enrol, indicating the day of the enrolment.)

2.) On the following feast days: Christmas, Easter, Annunciation, Purification, Assumption, Our Lady of the Rosary, and Immaculate Conception.

3.) For those who pray the Rosary, a plenary indulgence is granted under the usual conditions, when the Rosary is prayed in Church, or in a Public Oratory, in a family (family Rosary), Religious Community, or Pious Association. Otherwise a partial indulgence is granted. (EI 48)

4.) A partial indulgence is granted to those who use a Rosary blessed by a priest (see below in the section 'The Rosary Blessing), even if five decades are not recited. The indulgence is plenary on the feast of Sts. Peter and Paul, if the blessing was performed by the pope or a bishop. (following EI 35)

Where You May Enrol Online:

https://rosarycenter.org/enroll-in-the-rosary-confraternity

The Archconfraternity Prayer

(Required by Members)

Queen of the Most Holy Rosary and Mother of us all, we come to you for help in our sorrows, trials and necessities. Sin leaves us weak and helpless but Divine Grace heals and strengthens.

We ask for the grace to love Jesus as you loved Him, to believe as you believed, to hope as you hoped; we ask to share your purity of mind and heart. Give us true sorrow for sin and make us love people as you and Jesus loved them. Obtain for us the gifts of the Holy Spirit that we may be wise with your wisdom, understand with your understanding, know with your knowledge, be prudent with your prudence, be patient with your patience, be courageous with your fortitude and desire justice ardently for everyone with the all consuming desire of the Sacred Heart of Jesus your Son.

Open our minds that as we pray the Rosary we will understand the teachings of the Gospel contained in its mysteries.

We pray especially for the members of the Rosary Confraternity whom we love. Help them wherever they may be; guide them, watch over them and make them strong in their trials and suffering. We are drawn together by a common bond of great charity for you and for each other; keep us faithful to your Son and to your Rosary until death.

Intercede for the souls in Purgatory, especially for the members of the Rosary Confraternity who have died. May they rest in peace. Finally we ask for grace of final perseverance for ourselves and for our loved ones that we may all be reunited in heaven forever.

Saint Dominic, you who received so much Grace and Strength from the Rosary, pray for us. Amen.

Imprimi Potest:
Thomas P. Raftery O.P., Lect. S.Th., J.C.D.

Nihil Obstat:
  ✠ *Paul E. Waldschmidt CSC, D.D., S.T.D.*

Imprimatur:
  ✠ *Cornelius M. Power, D.D., J.C.D.*
Archbishop of Portland
March 30, 1979

The Rosary Blessing –
Including the Official Blessing

Until the promulgation of *Inter Oecumenici* in 1964, the blessing of Rosaries was a reserved blessing, and only priests of the Dominican Order could bless them. That is why the older Roman Rituals did not contain a blessing for Rosaries. Today any priest or deacon may bless a Rosary using forms in use from 1964 to 1984 or the form found in the new *Liber Benedictionum* of 1984 (LB 506):

Priest: May this Rosary and the one who uses it be blessed, in the name of the Father, and of the Son, ✠ and of the Holy Spirit.

R. Amen.

Dominican priests, however, may wish to use the blessings proper to the Order. The first of these is a longer formula which is especially suitable when blessing Rosaries for members of the Rosary Confraternity:

BLESSING OF ROSARIES: LONGER FORM

The priest wears a white stole, and says:

> *V. Our help is in the name of the Lord.*
> *R. Who made heaven and earth.*
> *V. The Lord be with you.*
> *R. And with your spirit.*

Let us Pray:

Almighty and merciful God, on account of your very great love for us, you willed that your only-begotten Son, our Lord Jesus Christ, should come down from heaven to earth, and at the angel's message take flesh in the most sacred womb of Our Lady, the most blessed Virgin Mary, submit to death on the cross, and then rise gloriously from the dead on the third day, in order to deliver us from Satan's tyranny. We humbly beg you, in your boundless goodness to bless ✠ and to sanctify ✠ these rosaries, which your faithful Church has consecrated to the honour and praise of the Mother of your Son. Let them be endowed with such power of the Holy Spirit, that whoever carries one on his person or reverently keeps one in his home, or devoutly prays to you while meditating on the divine mysteries, according to the rules of his holy society, may fully share in all the graces, privileges and indulgences which the Holy See has granted to this society. May he always and everywhere be shielded from all enemies, visible and invisible, and at his death deserve to be presented to you by the most blessed Virgin Mary herself, Mother of God. Through the same Lord Jesus Christ, your Son, who lives and reigns with you in the unity of the

Holy Spirit, God for ever and ever.

R. Amen.

The rosaries are then sprinkled with Holy Water.

When the blessing is not done for members of the Confraternity or when brevity is more suitable, the shorter formula may be used:

BLESSING OF ROSARIES: SHORT FORM

V. To the honour and glory of Mary, the Virgin Mother of God, in memory of the mysteries of the life, death, and resurrection of our Lord, the same Jesus Christ, may this crown of the most holy Rosary be blessed ✠ and sanctified ✠ in the name of the Father, ✠ and of the Son, and of the Holy Spirit.

R. Amen.

(If several Rosaries are blessed the plural is used; use of stole and holy water are optional.)

How to Pray the Rosary

The Rosary is a perfect combination of vocal and mental prayer, both of which are vital in the spiritual life of a Christian as salvation cannot be attained without prayer, and spiritual perfection cannot be obtained without meditative prayer as well as vocal.

The meditations of the Rosary focus on the Life, Passion, death, and triumph of Jesus Christ, and of course, the great graces given to the Mother of God, the promised Woman that would crush the head of the serpent.

The traditional Rosary devotion consists of three sets of 'mysteries', that is, 'mystical contemplations' – the Joyful Mysteries, the Sorrowful Mysteries, and the Glorious Mysteries.

While saying one set of mysteries is usually called a 'rosary', in fact, one whole Rosary consists of saying all three mysteries, but since not everyone can say the entire Rosary in a day, the devotion has been sectioned into days, with certain mysteries assigned to specific days.

* Monday and Thursday: the Joyful Mysteries.
* Tuesday and Friday: the Sorrowful Mysteries.
* Wednesday, Saturday and Sunday: the Glorious Mysteries.

However, with St. John Paul II's introduction of the new Luminous Mysteries circa. 2001-2002, the following pattern is now suggested:

* Monday and Saturday: the Joyful Mysteries.
* Thursday: the Luminous Mysteries
* Tuesday and Friday: the Sorrowful Mysteries
*Wednesday and Sunday: the Glorious Mysteries.

Note: if one does not wish to say the Luminous Mysteries, one may omit them without pain of sin, and say the three traditional mysteries.   This is also the same with the days suggested, they are not set in stone, and may be adapted according to prayer needs or certain feast days, etc. without pain of sin. The weekly pattern was adopted to ensure that those with the pious habit of saying a daily rosary would enable them to say an entire rosary at least once or twice a week.

For Rosary Archconfraternity members: saying one whole rosary each week is a requirement to participate in the special graces and indulgences granted to the confraternity. Currently, until future notice, members of the confraternity need not say the Luminous mysteries to fulfil their obligation to pray an entire rosary a week, but it is strongly encouraged. However, they are required to say the Confraternity Prayer with their rosaries, (see the section above.)

The Beads and Prayers:

When reciting the rosary, one must have their own set of rosary beads and follow with along with the beads as they pray. If there are several people saying it together, it is only necessary that one person hold a set of beads in order to keep count the number of prayers.[**] However, it is always good to hold your own set of blessed beads as they are a graced sacramental and terrify the demons.

1) **The Rosary is commenced with the Sign of the cross. Then, the Apostles Creed is said on the crucifix of the beads:**

[**]   This is according to the "The Catechism Explained; An Exhaustive Explanation of the Catholic Religion' by Spirago and Clarke, p. 694

"I believe in God, the Father Almighty, Creator of Heaven and earth; and in Jesus Christ, His only Son, Our Lord, Who was conceived by the Holy Ghost, born of the Virgin Mary, suffered under Pontius Pilate, was crucified, died, and was buried. He descended into hell: the third day He rose again from the dead; He ascended into Heaven and is seated at the right hand of God, the Father of Almighty; from thence He shall come to judge the living and the dead. I believe in the Holy Ghost, the holy Catholic Church, the communion of saints, the forgiveness of sins, the resurrection of the body, and the life of the world to come. Amen."

Then, an Our Father, three Hail Marys, and a Glory Be are said on the beads that come after. These Three Hail Marys are said in petition that the three theological virtues may be increased within us: Faith, Hope and Charity.[+]

2) Next, the five Mysteries of the particular day are contemplated upon in each of the five decades. **Each decade begins with an Our Father, ten Hail Marys, and concludes with the Glory Be.** After the approved apparitions of Our Lady of Fatima in 1917, upon her request, the following prayer has been added at the end of each decade after the Glory Be:

+ Ibid.

"O my Jesus, forgive us our sins, save us from the fires of Hell, lead all souls to Heaven, especially those most in need of Thy mercy."

In some countries there is a tradition of also concluding each decade with the prayer of the Miraculous Medal:

"O Mary, conceived without sin, pray for us who have recourse to thee."

3) The five decades are concluded with the Hail Holy Queen.

"Hail Holy Queen, Mother of Mercy, hail! Our life, our sweetness and our hope! To thee do we cry, poor banished children of Eve, to thee do we send up our sighs, mourning and weeping in this valley of tears. Turn then most gracious advocate, thine eyes of mercy towards us; and after this our exile, show unto us the blessed fruit of thy womb, Jesus. O clement, O loving, O sweet Virgin Mary!
P. Pray for us, O holy Mother of God,
R. That we may be made worthy of the promises of Christ."

This concluding set of prayers may also be said, which is optional:

"O God! Whose only-begotten Son, by His life, death and resurrection, has purchased for us the reward of eternal life; grant, we beseech Thee, that, meditating upon these mysteries of the most holy Rosary of the Blessed Virgin

Mary, we may imitate what they contain and obtain what they promise. Through the same Christ our Lord. Amen.

May the Divine assistance remain always with us. Amen. And may the souls of the faithful departed, through the mercy of God, rest in peace. Amen.

Holy Virgin, with thy loving Child, thy blessing give to us this day (or night.)

(Conclude with the sign of the cross):

In the name of the Father, and of the Son, and of the Holy Ghost. Amen.

The MYSTERIES

The Joyful Mysteries

1) The Annunciation
2) The Visitation
3) The Nativity
4) The Presentation of Christ at the Temple
5) The Finding of the Child Jesus in the Temple

The Sorrowful Mysteries

1) The Agony in the Garden
2) The Scourging at the Pillar
3) The Crowning with Thorns
4) The Carrying of the Cross
5) The Crucifixion

The Glorious Mysteries

1) The Resurrection
2) The Ascension
3) The Descent of the Holy Ghost at Pentecost
4) The Assumption of the Blessed Virgin
    into Heaven
5) The Coronation of the Blessed Virgin

The Luminous Mysteries

1) Christ's Baptism in the Jordan
2) The Wedding at Cana
3) Christ's Proclamation of the Kingdom
4) The Transfiguration on Mt. Tabor
5) The Institution of the Eucharist

ဏ❀ﭼﻼ❀ﭼﻼ❀ﻼ

The Three Hail Marys Devotion

This devotion was originally revealed to St. Mechtilde when she prayed to Our Lady for the grace of a happy death and asked that she would assist her in her last agony. Our Lady appeared to her and said;

"Dear Daughter, I will certainly. But I also want you to say three Hail Marys to me every day.

The first will be in honour of God the Father, Whose omnipotence raised my soul so high above every other creature that after God I have the greatest power in Heaven and on earth. In the hour of your death I will use that power of God the Father to keep any hostile power far from you.

The second Hail Mary will be said in honour of the Son of God Who communicated His inscrutable wisdom to me. In the hour of your death I will fill your soul with the light of that wisdom so that all the darkness of ignorance and error will be dispelled.

The third Hail Mary will be in honour of God the Holy Ghost Who filled my soul with the sweetness of His love, tenderness and mercy, so much so, that after God I am the sweetest and most merciful.

If you do that I promise you final perseverance. In your last hour I will then change the bitterness of death into divine sweetness and delight."

The same grace would also be given to those who practised this devotion.

St. Gertrude the Great, the novice of St. Mechtilde, also received revelations regarding this devotion. One day when she sang the Hail Mary at the matins of the Annunciation, she saw a vision of God:

from the Heart of the Father and of the Son, and of the Holy Ghost, she saw spring forth three bright flames which penetrated the Heart of the Holy Virgin. Then she heard the following words:

"After the Power of the Father, the Wisdom of the Son, and the merciful Tenderness of the Holy Spirit, nothing approaches the Power, the Wisdom and the merciful Tenderness of Mary." Our Lady told her: "To any soul who faithfully prays the Three Hail Marys I will appear at the hour of death in a splendour of beauty so extraordinary that it will fill the soul with Heavenly consolation."

St. Anthony of Padua took this devotion to heart. He was one of the first to practise it and recommended it to others. Through this devotion he desired to honour the virginity of Mary and to receive the grace of a pure mind, heart and body in the midst of the temptations and dangers of the world.

A Dominican nun in the 16th century named Mary Villana was devoted to this practise. One day she received a revelation from the Blessed Virgin:

"Not only will you obtain whatever it is that you ask me, provided it benefits your soul, but I promise you I will be a special protectress of whoever salutes me with this devotion." She added: "I have always been very pleased with the devotion of the three Hail Marys ... Never stop saying them and make them known to everyone ... You will verify the effectiveness of this devotion every day."

St. Alphonsus Liguori (1696-1787) also practised the Three Hail Marys, and also recommended that parents train their children to practise it, <u>not just once a day but twice</u>: saying three Hail Marys in the morning and also in the evening. <u>This practise of saying them twice a day is now part of the devotion.</u> St.

Alphonsus also added the prayer to each Hail Mary: *"By thy pure and Immaculate Conception, O Mary, make my body pure and my soul holy."*

St. Leonard of Port Maurice (1676-1751) also encouraged the practise of saying the Three Hail Marys each morning and evening to honour Immaculate Mary and to obtain the grace to avoid all mortal sins during the day and night. He was absolutely confident that anyone who was faithful to this practise could be assured of their eternal salvation.

The devotion was approved by Benedict XV on July 20, 1921, and raised to the dignity of an Archconfraternity. Pope Leo XIII further attached an indulgence of 200 days each recitation for those who practise this devotion, 300 days for members of the Archconfraternity.[++]

The spiritual fruits received from this devotion have included, extraordinary cures from infirmities, miraculous protection from dangers of all kinds, the grace to overcome severe temptations and bad habits, especially regarding sins of impurity, and also conversions and spiritual advancement.

[++] While anyone can practise this devotion to gain the graces promised by Our Lady, in order to gain the additional special blessings and indulgences granted to any Archconfraternity attached to a devotion, one must enrol and fulfil the required obligations listed. However, I have not been able to find any other information on this particular Archconfraternity established by Benedict XV in its original form and if it is still in existence. It is possible it was made defunct as another similar Archconfraternity was already in existence since 1876, the 'Confraternity of Our Lady of Perpetual Help and St. Alphonsus Liguori', the requirement for this confraternity is to say three Hail Marys in the morning and at night in addition to other obligations. This you may still be enrolled in. (E.A. Bucc.)

སྃ ✾ ལྃ

The Practise of the Devotion

For the Morning begin with:

"O my Mother, preserve me from mortal sin during this day."

For the Evening, begin with:

"O my Mother, preserve me from mortal sin during this night."

Next, say the following:

1) <u>In Honour of Our Lady's Power</u>

Oh, Immaculate Mary, Virgin most powerful, I beseech thee, through that immense power which thou hast received from the Eternal Father, obtain for me purity of heart, strength to overcome all the enemies of my soul, and the special favour I implore in my present necessity. (Name your request). Mother most pure! Forsake me not, despise not my prayer, graciously hear me for God's glory, thy honour, and the welfare of my soul.

To obtain this favour I honour thy power by reciting: **Hail Mary, etc.** Then: "By thy pure and Immaculate Conception, O Mary, make my body pure and my soul holy, preserve me this day (or this night) from mortal sin. "

2. In Honour of Our Lady's Wisdom

Oh Virgin Mary, my Mother, through that ineffable wisdom bestowed upon thee by the Incarnate Word of God, I humbly beseech thee, obtain for me meekness and humility of heart, a perfect knowledge of the Divine Will, and strength to accomplish it always. Oh Mary, Seat of Wisdom; as a tender Mother lead me in the path of Christian virtue and perfection; enlighten and enable me to do what is most pleasing to thy beloved Son, and obtain my petition.

To obtain this favour I honour thy wisdom by reciting: **Hail Mary, etc.** Then: "By thy pure and Immaculate Conception, O Mary, make my body pure and my soul holy, preserve me this day (or this night) from mortal sin."

3. In Honour of Our Lady's Mercy

Oh, Mother of Mercy, Mother of penitent sinners, I stand before thee sinful and sorrowful, beseeching thee through the immense Love given to thee by the Holy Spirit for us poor sinners, obtain for me true and perfect contrition for my sins, which I hate and detest with all my heart, because I love God. Mother most merciful, help me in my present necessity. Turn, then those eyes of mercy toward us, oh clement, oh loving, oh sweet Virgin Mary!

To obtain this favour I honour thy mercy by reciting: **Hail Mary, etc.** Then: "By thy pure and Immaculate Conception, O Mary, make my body pure and my soul holy, preserve me this day (or this night) from mortal sin."

Conclude by saying a **Glory Be,** then: "Mary, by thy Immaculate Conception, purify my body and sanctify my soul."

ഇ❀ଓഇ❀ଓഇ❀ଓ

O Gloriosa Domina

O Gloriosa Domina is the second half of the hymn *Quem terra, pontus, aethera* which was composed by Venantius Fortunatus (530-609 AD), who was Bishop of Poitiers.

In 1224 at the Franciscan Monastery of Alenquer, Portugal, a novice had committed a fault that he needed to confess to the Master of Novices, and as customary the Master was required to give him a penance.

However, it is said the Master ordered him not to leave the altar of Our Lady in the Chapter Hall until the Mother of God had revealed to him the prayer that pleased her the most. Perhaps the Master suspected the novice of having some special favour or grace with Our Lady and wanted to test the humility and obedience of the novice, or to see if Our lady would really answer him, perhaps both.

After receiving this penance, the novice proceeded to pray all day on his knees before the altar, and well into the night. Finally he begged Our Lady in all humility to please answer the request demanded by his superior, which it was his duty to obey, and that he would not leave until he received an answer.

The statue on the altar than leaned towards him and spoke:

"Go, beloved son, and tell your Master that the hymn *O Gloriosa Domina* that the Church sings to me is, amongst all the prayers, the one that most pleases me. And to prove that what I say you is true, this, my Infant, who until now I held in my right arm, I now pass to my left arm. For this reason, you may go with confidence and give my response, for when all will see such an extraordinary marvel, they will believe what you say. So go, and invite the Master and the other religious to come visit me."

The novice thanked Our Lady and immediately told the Master. The religious of the monastery all saw the miracle, that the Child had changed position and was firmly in her other arm. After this great privilege was granted to the novice and also to them, the miraculous statue of Our Lady was named Our Lady of Privileges.

News of this spread, and it is assumed St. Anthony had heard of this and why it became his favourite hymn, while other stories say he heard it from his own mother. He not only sang it on his death-bed, but also when the devil tried to attack him by drowning him, but the holy saint put the demon to flight by singing this hymn.[36]

---

36 Research on the miraculous history of the hymn by Prof. Plinio Corrêa de Oliveira. Source: Tradition in Action: https://traditioninaction.org/SOD/j334_Pri_1_9.htm

The Hymn

O gloriosa domina
excelsa super sidera,
qui te creavit provide,
lactas sacrato ubere.

Quod Eva tristis abstulit,
tu reddis almo germine;
intrent ut astra flebiles,
sternis benigna semitam.

Tu regis alti ianua
et porta lucis fulgida;
vitam datam per Virginem,
gentes redemptae, plaudite.

Patri sit Paraclito
tuoque Nato gloria,
qui veste te mirabili
circumdederunt gratiae.   Amen.

Translation:

O Heaven's glorious mistress,
enthron'd above the starry sky!
thou feedest with thy sacred breast
thy own Creator, Lord most high.

What man had lost in hapless Eve,
thy sacred womb to man restores,
thou to the wretched here beneath
hast open'd Heaven's eternal doors.

Hail, O refulgent Hall of light!
Hail Gate august of Heaven's High King!
through thee redeem'd to endless life,
thy praise let all the nations sing.

To the Father and the Spirit
and to thy Son all glory be,
who with a wondrous garment
of graces encircled thee. Amen.

The Complete Message
of Our Lady of La Salette

Excerpt from 'The Sun Her Mantle' by John Beevers, (Browne and Nolan, LTD / The Richview Press, Dublin 1953).

ഓ✾ങ

"Come nearer, my children. Don't be afraid. I have come to give you important news.

If my people will not submit I shall be compelled to let go the arm of my Son. It is so heavy and so powerful that I can no longer sustain it. For how long have I suffered on your behalf! If I do not want my Son to abandon you, I must pray to Him ceaselessly, though you take no account of it.

Pray as much as you like, do as much as you like, but you will never be able to repay me for the trouble I have taken over you.

I have given you six days in which to work. I have reserved the seventh for Myself and yet you do not wish to let Me have it. (*Observation: it is apparent Our Lady is quoting a message from Our Lord. E.A. Bucc*)

The carters never swear without using the Name of my Son. These are the two things which are weighing down so heavily the arm of my Son.

If the harvest is spoilt, it is only because of you. Last year, I showed you this in the potato crop, but you took no notice. On the contrary, when you saw the spoilt potatoes, you swore, using the name of my Son. The potatoes will go on rotting and, by Christmas this year, there will be none."

The children did not understand her. Mélanie could not grasp what what *pommes de terre* (potatoes) meant. The only *pommes* she knew grew on apple trees. She looked puzzled and turned to Maximin to see if he could explain.

The Lady checked her.

"Can't you understand, my children? I will tell you in different words."

And she repeated the message about the harvest in the local *patois*, speaking it as easily as if she had been born and bred in the district. She continued, still using the *patois*.

"If you have wheat, do not sow it, for pests will devour all that you sow, and any of it that ripens will fall to dust when it is threshed. A great famine will come. Before it comes, little children under seven will be seized with a palsy and will die in the arms of those carrying them. The rest of the people will suffer their penance through the famine. The nuts will be grub-ridden and the grapes will rot."

At this point, Mélanie ceased to hear the Lady's voice, although she saw her lips move and Maximin listening with great attention. Then she heard the voice again, but it was silent for Maximin. As she spoke to Mélanie, Maximin behaved like a bored child, taking off his hat and twirling it round on the end of his stick, or flicking the pebbles at his feet with the stick and sending them rolling to the feet of the Lady.

The voice resumed for the both of them:

"If the people change their hearts, the stones and the rocks will turn into heaps of wheat and the fields will sow themselves with potatoes. Do you say your prayers well, my children?"

They both answered: "Hardly at all."

"Ah, my children, you must say at least an Our Father and a Hail Mary. When you can, say more. During the summer, only a few elderly women go to Mass. The rest of the people work in the fields throughout Sunday in the summer. In the winter, when they have nothing to do, they go to Mass only to jeer at religion. And in Lent, they go to the butchers as if they were dogs."

(Observations: to place this in context, this message was given after France had suffered the Masonically-influenced anti-Catholic French Revolution, which had introduced the secular state, decimating the former piety and religious observance among the populace in many places in France. For example, we see around this time the Curé of Ars turned his irreligious and spiritually decrepit parish into a spiritual haven, which he only accomplished through a lifetime of heroic efforts of austere sacrifice and penance, battling against the very vices of the morally decrepit populace mentioned by Our Lady above. E.A. Bucc.)

Our Lady: "Have you ever seen spoilt wheat, my children?"

They both said they had not.

She turned to Maximin.

"But my child, you certainly saw it once – when you went with your father to Coin (a hamlet near Corps). There was a man there who asked your father to go with him and see his ruined wheat. He went, took

230

two or three of the ears of wheat and rubbed them in his hand. They crumbled to dust. On your way back, when you were still half-an-hour's walk from Corps, your father gave you a bit of bread and said 'Here child, you can still eat bread this year, but, if things go on like this, we don't know who will eat it next year.' "

"That's right, Madame," exclaimed Maximin. "I didn't remember it as first, but I do now." He remembered going to Coin with his father to buy an ash-tree. Everything had happened as the Lady said. Now came her final words:

"Well, my children, spread this message among all my people."

She spoke this in French, and them moved forward, Maximin stepping aside to let her pass. She crossed the Spezia, brushing a great stone which had been rolled into the stream to make an easy crossing-place when the water was high with the melting snows. After she had gone a few yards, she spoke again without turning around, repeating with a little more emphasis her final word to the children:

"Be sure, My children, to spread this message among all my people."

଼ଵ ✿ ଵ଼

John Beevers notes the prophecies regarding the famine came to pass, the following excerpt is also from "The Sun Her Mantle", (pp. 108-109):

"(Our Lady) spoke of the recent bad potato crop and declared that the potatoes would continue to rot. They did and not only in France. The winter of 1846 saw Ireland ravaged by the great potato famine. A secular historian has said that a characteristic of the pestilence which impressed all observers was "the universal, infiltrating stench of the rotting plants. This smell of the charnel house went for to induce many of the peasantry, and still more of their social superiors, to believe that they were confronted by no ordinary trouble, but that this was a visitation from on high, a scourge to punish the sins of the people." The Census Commission of 1851 estimated that about a million of Ireland's people died of famine. The next year, 1847, March 24 was observed throughout the United Kingdom with very great solemnity, for it was appointed by Royal Proclamation as a day of "general fast and humiliation before Almighty God, in order to obtain the pardon of our sins, and that we may, in the most devout and solemn manner, send up our prayers and supplications to the Divine Majesty for the removal of those heavy judgements which our manifold sins have most justly deserved, and which Almighty God is pleased to visit the iniquities of this land by a grievous scarcity and dearth of divers articles of sustenance and necessaries of life."

In the winter of the same year, 200,000 people in Scotland had to be given food from the State to enable them to live to the next harvest. Nearly a fifth of the population of Belgium were getting food from charitable organisations. There were food riots in Belgium, France and England. In France, 72,000 people died in 1854 and another 80,000 the next year – all of starvation. All Europe was short of food, not only because of potato blight, but because of abnormally bad grain harvests – also prophesied by Our Lady.

She also warned that children would die and this, too, was fulfilled in the great outbreak of cholera in which hundreds of thousands died, the majority of them children. In 1849, there were 53,000 deaths from cholera in England and Wales and some 30,000 in Ireland. In 1854, 150,000 people died of cholera in France. During these five years 1849-54, it is reckoned that in Europe, including Russia, some three-quarters of a million people died from cholera.

Our Lady spoke of the plague that was to rot the grapes. It duly came at the end of the 1860s in the shape of phylloxera which, between 1870 and 1905, laid waste practically every vineyard in Europe."

ℴ❄℞

The Original Secrets of La Salette sent to Bl Pius IX in 1851.

(About these texts: they were rediscovered in 1999 in the Vatican archives by Fr Michel Corteville. He published the texts of the secrets complete with images of the letters and the original envelopes in which they were sent by the two seers of La Salette. [37]

His publication of the original Secrets cannot be a hoax as his image of the letters complete with childish handwriting, various misspellings and the envelopes all match eyewitness descriptions of the letters that were sent to the Pope. ~E.A. Bucc)

ഇ✵ര

MAXIMIN'S FIRST VERSION OF HIS SECRET:

On September 19, 1846, we saw a beautiful Lady. We never said that this lady was the Blessed Virgin but we always said that it was a beautiful Lady.

I do not know if it is the Blessed Virgin or another person. As for me, I believe today that it is the Blessed Virgin. Here is what this Lady said to me:

---

37 *"Discovery of the Secret of La Salette"*, by Fathers René Laurentin and Michel Corteville, (Fayard Publications, April 2002)

"If my people continue, what I will say to you will arrive earlier, if it changes a little, it will be a little later.

France has corrupted the universe, one day it will be punished. The faith will die out in France: three quarters of France will not practice religion any more, or almost no more, the other part will practice it without really practising it. Then, after [that], nations will convert, the faith will be rekindled everywhere.

A great country, now Protestant, in the north of Europe, will be converted; by the support of this country all the other nations of the world will be converted.

Before all that arrives, great disorders will arrive, in the Church, and everywhere. Then, after [that], our Holy Father the Pope will be persecuted. His successor will be a pontiff that nobody expects.

Then, after [that], a great peace will come, but it will not last a long time. A monster will come to disturb it.

All that I tell you here will arrive in the other century, at the latest in the year two thousand."

Maximin Giraud

(She told me to say it some time before.)

My Most Holy Father, your holy blessing to one of your sheep.

Grenoble, July 3, 1851.

235

ဆ ✿ ဢ

MELANIE'S FIRST VERSION OF HER SECRET

J.M.J.

Secret which the Blessed Virgin gave me on the Mountain of La Salette on September 19, 1846 Secr[e]t.

Mélanie, I will say something to you which you will not say to anybody:
The time of God's wrath has arrived!

If, when you say to the people what I have said to you so far, and what I will still ask you to say, if, after that, they do not convert, (if they do not do penance, and they do not cease working on Sunday, and if they continue to blaspheme the Holy Name of God), in a word, if the face of the earth does not change, God will be avenged against the people ungrateful and slave of the demon.

My Son will make His power manifest! Paris, this city soiled by all kinds of crimes, will perish infallibly. Marseilles will be destroyed in a little time. When these things arrive, the disorder will be complete on the earth, the world will be given up to its impious passions. The pope will be persecuted from all sides, they will shoot at him, they will want to put him to death, but no one will not be able to do it, the Vicar of God will triumph again this time.

The priests and the Sisters, and the true servants of my Son will be persecuted, and several will die for the faith of Jesus-Christ. A famine will reign at the same time.

After all these will have arrived, many will recognize the hand of God on them, they will convert, and do penance for their sins.

A great king will go up on the throne, and will reign a few years. Religion will re-flourish and spread all over the world, and there will be a great abundance, the world, glad not to be lacking nothing, will fall again in its disorders, will give up God, and will be prone to its criminal passions

God's ministers, and the Spouses of Jesus-Christ, there will be some who will go astray, and that will be the most terrible.

Lastly, hell will reign on earth. It will be then that the Antichrist will be born of a Sister, but woe to her! Many will believe in him, because he will claim to have come from heaven, woe to those who will believe in him!

That time is not far away, twice 50 years will not go by.

My child, you will not say what I have just said to you. (You will not say it to anybody, you will not say if you must say it one day, you will not say what that it concerns), finally you will say nothing anymore until I tell you to say it!

I pray to Our Holy Father the Pope to give me his holy blessing.

Mélanie Mathieu,
Shepherdess of La Salette, Grenoble, July 6, 1851.

J.M.J.

+

MAXIMIN'S SECOND VERSION

(A few weeks after the first version of the Secret were sent to Bl Pius IX, Benjamin Dausse, who witnessed Maximin and Mélanie write their letters, asked Maximin if he would send him some remembrance of the event. Maximin surprisingly answered the request by writing the secret down again in a letter to him dated August 11, 1851 – EA. Bucc.)

"On 19 September 1846, I saw a lady bright as the sun, I believe to be the Blessed Virgin. But I never said it was the Blessed Virgin. I've always said that I had seen a beautiful lady, but never the Blessed Virgin. It is the Church to judge by what I will say if this is truly the Holy Virgin or anyone else for what I will say here after. She told me in the middle of the story, after the grapes will rot and nuts will spoil. She began by telling me:

If my people are not converted what I say will happen sooner, otherwise it will happen later. Three quarters of France will lose the Faith and the other quarter will practice it with lukewarmness; then afterwards the Faith will reappear in France. A Northern country, now Protestant, will be converted, and with the support of this country the other nations will convert. There will come a peace, and after that peace there will come a monster who will disturb the peace, and peace will come when all nations will be converted. The Pope's successor will be someone that nobody expects. He will not be Roman (written in the margin). The monster will come during the peace, and peace and the monster will come in the 19th or 20th century at the latest. You will not tell this to anyone. You will not tell this to anyone. This is all She told me.

Maximin Giraud, shepherd
August 11, 1851 at Grenoble.

(OBSERVATIONS of importance regarding the dating: Benjamin Dausse declared that at the time of this writing Maximin was still somewhat unlearned, the education he received after the apparition at La Salette was still basic at this point, and Dausse was of the opinion Maximin believed he was living in the 18th rather than in the 19th century. Therefore, the timing Maximin gave regarding the fulfilment of the prophecy could be corrected to read "20th or 21st century.")

෨❀ဢ෨❀ဢ෨❀ဢ

The Devotion of the Seven Sorrows

St. Bridget of Sweden (1303-1373) was graced with numerous visitations from heaven, many times she saw the Blessed Virgin. One of the simplest and most beautiful devotions that was revealed to her was that of the Seven Sorrows. The Mother of God declared she would grant seven graces to the souls who honour her daily by saying seven Hail Marys and meditating on her tears and dolours.

The Seven Graces:

I will grant peace to their families.

They will be enlightened about the Divine Mysteries.

I will console them in their pains and I will accompany them in their work.

I will give them as much as they ask for, as long as it does not oppose the Adorable Will of my Divine Son, or the sanctification of their souls.

I will defend them in their spiritual battles with the infernal enemy. I will protect them at every instant of their lives.

I will visibly help them at the moment of their death, they will see the face of their Mother.

I have obtained this grace from my Divine Son, that those who propagate this devotion to my tears and sorrows, will be taken directly from this earthly life to eternal happiness since all their sins will be forgiven and my Son and I will be their eternal consolation and joy.

The Seven Sorrows:

1) The prophecy of Simeon.

2) The flight into Egypt.

3) The loss of the Child Jesus in the temple.

4) The meeting of Jesus and Mary on the Way of the Cross.

5) The Crucifixion.

6) The taking down of the Body of Jesus from the Cross.

7) The burial of Jesus.

REFUGIUM PECCATORUM

VENEZ TOUS À MOI, ET JE VOUS PROTÉGERAI

COR MARIÆ
IMMACULATUM

The Salutation to Mary
by St. John Eudes

This beautiful salutation was composed by St. John Eudes (1601-1680), and was said by St. Margaret Mary (1647-1690) as a copy of them were found in her prayer book.

The devotion was propagated by the Benedictine Fr. Paul de Moll (1824-1896) of Belgium. Early in his religious life he became very ill and was on the point of death. Our Lord, together with Our Lady and also St. Benedict to whom Fr. de Moll was devoted, also appeared. Our Lord said, "Be healed! ... I will grant all you ask of Me for others." After this, his prayers became very efficacious and people flocked to him for his prayers. He had a reputation for sanctity and also of working miracles in addition to giving various prophetic sayings. After his death, his body was found to be incorrupt.

This was a favourite devotion of his for he said: "This Salutation is so beautiful, recite it daily. From her throne in Heaven the Blessed Virgin will bless you and you must make the sign of the Cross. Yes! If only you could see – Our Lady blesses you. I know it!" He also said, "Offered for the conversion of a sinner it would be impossible not to be granted."

Hail Mary! Daughter of God the Father.
Hail Mary! Mother of God the Son.
Hail Mary! Spouse of God the Holy Spirit.

Hail Mary! Temple of the Most Blessed Trinity.
Hail Mary! Pure Lily of the Effulgent Trinity.
Hail Mary! Celestial Rose of
     the ineffable Love of God.
Hail Mary! Virgin pure and humble,
      of whom the King of Heaven willed to be born
        and with thy milk to be nourished.
Hail Mary! Virgin of virgins.
Hail Mary! Queen of Martyrs,
     whose soul a sword transfixed.
Hail Mary! Lady most blessed, unto whom
     all power in Heaven and earth is given.
Hail Mary! My Queen and my Mother!
     My life, my sweetness and my hope.
Hail Mary! Mother most amiable.
Hail Mary! Mother most admirable.
Hail Mary! Mother of Divine Love.
Hail Mary, Immaculate! Conceived without sin!
Hail Mary, Full of Grace, The Lord is with thee!
     Blessed art thou among women and blessed is
      the Fruit of thy womb, Jesus!
Blessed be thy spouse, St. Joseph.
Blessed be thy father, St. Joachim.
Blessed be thy mother, St. Anne.
Blessed be thy guardian, Saint John.
Blessed be thy holy angel, St. Gabriel.
Glory be to God the Father, Who chose thee.
Glory be to God the Son, Who loved thee.
Glory be to God the Holy Spirit, Who espoused thee.
O Glorious Virgin Mary,
     May all men love and praise thee.
Holy Mary, Mother of God, Pray for us
     and bless us, now and at death,
      in the Name of Jesus, thy Divine Son. Amen.

Illustration Credits

Page 28, *"Virgin and Child with an Angel"*, (c. 1475- 1485), Sandro Botticelli. Art Institute of Chicago. Public Domain.

Page 35, *"The Rebuke of Adam and Eve"*, (1740). Charles Joseph Natoire. Oil on copper. Metropolitan Museum. Public Domain.

Page 38, *"Allegory of the Immaculate Conception with the Fall of Man"*, (1578-1649), Alessandro Turchi. Pen and brown ink, brown wash, over traces of black chalk. Metropolitan Museum. Public Domain.

Page 42, *"Birth of the Virgin"*, (c. 1590 - c. 1595), Filippo Bellini. Rijksmuseum. Public Domain.

Page 49, *"The Presentation of the Virgin Mary"*, (1590–ca. 1620), Anonymous. Publisher: Justus Sadeler (Netherlandish, Antwerp ca. 1572/83–ca. 1620 Leiden). Metropolitan Museum. Public Domain.

Page 53, *"Saint Mary (the Blessed Virgin)"*, etching after O. Marinari, (1627-1715, or 1716). Wellcome Collection. Public Domain.

Page 56, *"Head of the Virgin looking up to the right, after Reni"*, (1869). Engraved by Robert Trossin. Metropolitan Museum. Public Domain.

Page 61, *"Annunciation to the Virgin"*, (1660 – 1680), Bartolomé Esteban Murillo. Rijksmuseum. Public Domain.

Page 70, *"The Visitation"*, (1498?-1554), Moretto da Brescia. Frick Digital Collections. Public Domain Photoarchive.

Page 75, "*The Magnificat*", (1444 or 1445-1510), Sandro Botticelli. Frick Digital Collections. Public Domain Photoarchive.

Page 82, "*The Adoration of the Magi*", (1526), Quinten Massys. Metropolitan Museum. Public Domain.

Page 86, "*The Presentation in the Temple*", (c. 1707–1768), Stefano Pozzi. Art Institute of Chicago. Public Domain.

Page 91, "*The Virgin of Sorrows*", (18th century), Anonymous. Spanish Colonial, Possibly made in Mexico. Metropolitan Museum. Public Domain.

Page 94, "*The flight into Egypt, the Virgin and Child on a donkey, Joseph to the left*," after Luca Giordano, (ca. 1765–93), by José del Castillo. Metropolitan Museum. Public Domain.

Page 99, "*Christus bij de leraren in de tempel*", (1728), after Arnold Houbraken, by Abraham de Blois. Rijksmuseum. Public Domain.

Page 102, "*Kruisdraging*", *(Christ carrying the cross)*, anonymous engraving, after Cornelis Galle (I), after Anthony van Dyck, 1615 – 1650. Rijksmuseum. Public Domain.

Page 106, "*The Crucifixion of Christ*", line engraving by J. Neeffs after Rubens, (c. 16--). Wellcome Collection. Public Domain.

Page 112, "*The Lamentation*", (1593), Scipione Pulzone (Il Gaetano). Metropolitan Museum. Public Domain.

Page 116, *"La Vierge au sepulcre"*, etching after Annibale Carracci (1560–1609), by Jean Morin (1605–1650, Paris). Metropolitan Museum. Public Domain.

Page 125, *"The Death of the Virgin"*, (1639), etching, by Rembrandt van Rijn. Rijksmuseum. Public Domain.

Page 128, *"The Death of the Virgin"*, (1485), Bartolomeo Vivarini. Metropolitan Museum. Public Domain.

Page 133, *"The Assumption of the Virgin"*, (1577–79), El Greco (Doménikos Theotokópoulos).   Art Institute of Chicago. Public Domain.

Page 137, *"Two sleeping cowherds on the Mont-sous-les-Baisses just before an appearance of the Virgin of the Salette"*, lithograph after F. Benoist (1818-1868) by E. Ciceri and Ph. Benoist. Wellcome Collection. Public Domain.

Page 141, *"Saint Mary (the Blessed Virgin)"*. Lithograph of La Salette. Wellcome Collection. Public Domain.

Page 144, *"The Virgin Mary with the Christ child, saints and martyrs (known as the 'Madonna del Rosario')*. Drawing after D. Zampieri, il Domenichino, (1619-21), by F. Rosaspina(c. 1830). Wellcome Collection Public Domain.

Page 147, *"Maria de Onbevlekte Ontvangenis verschijnt aan Bernadette Soubirous in een grot te Lourdes"*, (Apparition at Lourdes), engraving, anonymous, (1862 – 1866). Rijksmuseum. Public Domain.

Page 150, (*St. Bernadette, as a Young Girl, at the Time of Her Visions*). Anonymous, French School, active 19th century. Said to have been painted in 1858. Frick Digital Collections. Public Domain Photoarchive.

Page 152, *"Saint Mary (the Blessed Virgin) with the Christ Child."* Engraving by S.A. Bolswert after Sir P.P. Rubens. Wellcome Collection. Public Domain.

Page 159, *"Mother and Daughter in Prayer"*, (ca. 1811–17), Julius Schnorr von Carolsfeld. Metropolitan Museum. Public Domain.

Page 164, Luna Retable (Part XI: *Saint Thomas à Becket*). (1488). Sancho de Zamora, (active 1483-1495). Frick Digital Collection. Public Domain Photoarchive.

Page 175, *"The Virgin standing facing front and holding the infant Christ, angels behind them in the clouds"*, (ca 1700–1800). Metropolitan Museum. Public Domain.

Page 176, *"The Virgin of Carmen (Carmel) and the Souls of Purgatory with St. Joseph and the Prophet Elijah"*, (ca. 1720), Juan Francisco de Aguilera. Metropolitan Museum. Public Domain.

Page 193, *"Madonna and Child"*, (1500 – 1523), Borgognone. Rijksmuseum. Public Domain.

Page 216, *"The Virgin Mary"*, lithograph by S. Wiedenbauer after G. Salvi, il Sassoferrato, (1609-1685). Wellcome Collection. Public Domain.

Page 224, *"Saint Antony of Padua"*, engraving by F. Bartolozzi after A. Balestra, (1666-1740). Wellcome Collection. Public Domain.

Page 240, *"Saint Mary (the Blessed Virgin)"*, engraving by Jeronimus Wierix, (1553-1619). Public Domain.

Page 243, *"Saint Mary (the Blessed Virgin)."* Etching. Wellcome Collection, Reference 10258i. Public Domain.

**If you liked this book by Fr. Marin de Boylesve,
you will also like these:**

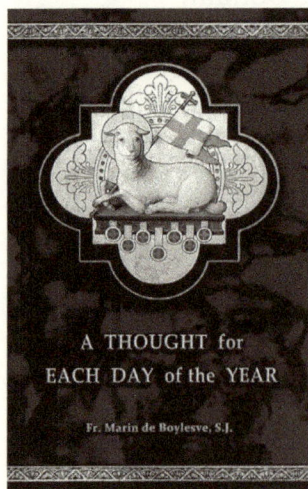

**A Thought for
Each Day of the Year**

ISBN: 978-989-33-1995-6

**Little Month
of Saint Joseph**

ISBN: 978-989-96844-8-5

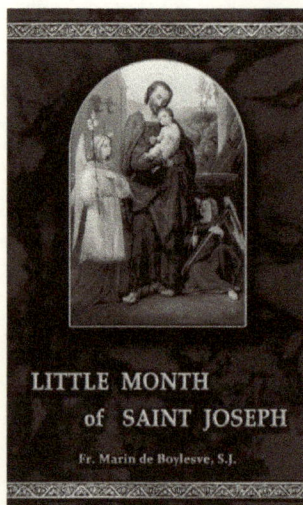

The Sacred Heart
of Jesus

ISBN: 978-989-33-2807-1

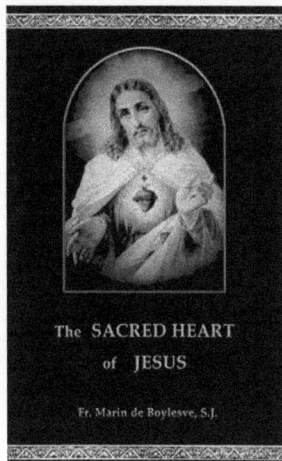

The Month
of the Precious Blood

ISBN: 978-989-33-2808-8

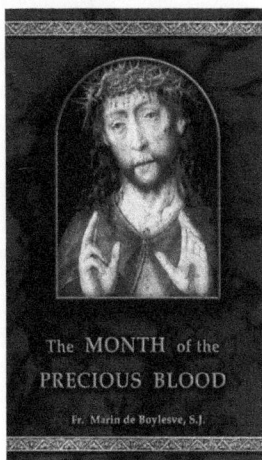

The Month
of Saint Michael

ISBN: 978-989-96844-9-2

www.ingramcontent.com/pod-product-compliance
Lightning Source LLC
Chambersburg PA
CBHW021049090426
42738CB00006B/258